ACTS

of the

GENERAL CHAPTER OF DIFFINITORS

of the

THE ORDER OF FRIAR PREACHERS

TROGIR

July 22 to August 8, 2013

CELEBRATED UNDER

FR. BRUNO CADORÉ

DOCTOR OF SACRED THEOLOGY

MASTER OF THE ORDER

CAPITVLVM
GENERALE ORDINIS
PRAEDICATORVM
TRAGVRII MMXIII

ROME

CURIA GENERALITIA – SANTA SABINA

ACKNOWLEDGEMENTS

We gratefully acknowledge the assistance of Fr. Paul Philibert, O.P., and Br. Cristobal de la Encarnacion Torres Iglesias of the Province of St. Martin de Porres, U.S.A. and Fr. Richard Peddicord, O.P., of the Province of St. Albert the Great, U.S.A. for their assistance with translations of French and Spanish texts; Fr. Albert Judy, O.P., of the Province of St. Albert the Great, U.S.A., for formatting and editing; Fr. Augustine Thompson, O.P. of the Province of the Holy Name, U.S.A., for proofreading Chapter X; and Fr. Andy McAlpin, O.P., of the Province of St. Albert the Great, U.S.A., and Managing Editor of the New Priory Press for production assistance.

Contents

vi

ACRONYMS

ACG	Acta Capituli Generalis
BEST	La Bible en Ses Traditions
BEST	La Bible en Ses Traditions
CIC	Codex Iuris Canonici
CIDALC	Conferencia Interprovincial Dominicana de América Latina y el Caribe
DSI	Dominican Sisters International
DVI	Dominican Volunteers International
DYM	Dominican Youth Movement (See IDYM)
EBAF	École Biblique et Archéologique Française
IAOP	Inter Africa O.P.
IDEO	Institut Dominicain d"Études Orientales - Cairo
IDF	International Dominican Foundation
IDYM	International Dominican Youth Movement = MJDI
IEOP	Inter Europe O.P.
ISOP	Instituto Storico O.P.
JIP	Junta Ibérica de Provinciales
LCO	Liber Constitutionum et Ordinationum fratrum O.P.
OPTIC	Order of Preachers for Technology, Information and Communication
PUST	Pontificia Università San Tommaso d'Aquino - Roma
RSG	*Ratio Studiorum Generalis*
STM	Master of Sacred Theology

Dear Brothers in Saint Dominic,

By means of this letter, I now promulgate the Acts of the General Chapter of Trogir (Croatia) held between July 22 and August 8, 2013. This chapter is one stage in the preparation for the celebration of the 800th anniversary of the confirmation of the Order, and the chapter's *Proemium* interprets these Acts in the light of the Jubilee. The capitulars accordingly chose to take as their theme: "Sent to Preach the Gospel."

A twofold approach was proposed to address this occasion of our Jubilee: *An approach of gratitude* for the gift of the Order's vocation, for the Lord's confidence in us and his faithfulness to us, for the tradition that has been handed down to us, for the richness and the diversity with which today's friars accomplish the preaching mission, and for the new vocations that we have been given. *An approach of truth and humility* drawing from the sources of our history and our tradition in a spirit of gratitude and *metanoia*, we beg the Lord to renew the generosity and the interior freedom that will ready us once again to be sent out to proclaim the Gospel with passion, creativity and joy, just as the first brothers of Dominic did.

At the heart of this approach is listening to the Word of God—in contemplation and in celebration, in study and in fraternal life, in dialogue with the world and in preaching. Through this individual and communal attention to the Word, we affirm our desire to allow the Spirit make our communities even deeper communities of faith and to conform our lives to the life of Christ. We affirm our desire to live this mystery, imitating the first witnesses to Jesus' own preaching, as persons configured to "the tenderness and the humanity of Christ" [from the Solemn Blessing for the Feast of St. Dominic in the Dominican Missal]. Such is the source of the renewed enthusiasm, joy, and creativity of men and women sent to be "witnesses to the resurrection." It is also the source from which we can draw the bold spirit to be witnesses and servants of God's friendship for the world, and to hope for a future of peace and communion in the world.

It is from the heart of our contemplation of the mystery of the generosity and grace of God that we are sent to preach the Gospel. We desire to respond to this mission with renewed zeal, *in medio Ecclesiae* [in the midst of the Church], along with many other Christians, particularly with the whole Dominican family, who want to become who they are meant to be by proclaiming the Gospel so that the Church of Christ may grow more fully. Sent as preachers under the banner of brotherhood, listening to our neighbors and in dialogue with them, we desire to bear witness to the mission of the Son of God himself, and to serve the charism of preaching in the Church.

Given this conviction, the chapter chose to draw the attention of all our friars and communities to certain concrete aspects of our life, inviting us to *take advantage of this time of preparation for our Jubilee as a chance to strengthen the life and mission of the Order*. Far from being merely an ephemeral self-celebration, the chapter proposes that the approach of the Jubilee should be a pathway – *a "school" – of truth and humility*, a pathway to *metanoia* that invites us as individuals and as communities to reinvest the full weight of meaning in each of the dimensions and in all of the demands of the life that we profess. In begging God for the *grace to be consecrated to the Word*, we desire that the encounter with and *listening to the Word of Life will transform us*, will become the source and the energy of the renewal of our Christian and Dominican life, and will stimulate our passion to preach the Gospel. This is our "school of life," and this is why, even though the chapter pays special attention to initial formation, it decidedly sees formation as a necessity that requires all of us to be caught up in a global dynamic of permanent formation through which we can choose to make ourselves day by day more attentive in listening to the Word. The path of *metanoia*, then, begins with the *determination of each one of us to reinvigorate the energy of his or her vocation*. It continues with the *common will to build up our fraternal communion* through a shared concern to construct really authentic communities such as the constitutions call us to be, through liturgical celebration, dialogue, study, apostolic sharing, simplicity of life and a truly communal stewardship of temporal goods, compassion for the most vulnerable, and forgiveness. All these demands of our life remind us that the brotherhood has been given to us by Dominic as the modality by which the Preachers desire to follow Christ.

Further, pursuing the process begun by the General Chapter of Rome in 2010, this chapter confirmed the need to *include in this process of renewal a better adaptation of some of the Order's structures for mission*, seeking to give to the friars and to communities conditions for the best possible apostolic creativity. The chapter also insists that priority be genuinely given to the *dynamic of formation*, both for the older brothers as well as for the new ones. Insisting on the primacy of fraternity, the chapter calls for respect for the *particular vocation of the cooperator brother* and for the promotion of that vocation, so important in underlining the value of the lay vocation to evangelization at the heart of the brotherhood of preachers.

The suppression of the "general vicariates" and "regional vicariates" for the sake of organizing the Order into Provinces (or Vice Provinces) and provincial vicariates should help to avoid the administrative burdens hindering the freedom and mobility needed for preaching in today's world, and at the same time it should foster dynamism and solidarity in the apostolate. In fact, this reform reveals our need *to clarify and consolidate the responsibility of Provinces with respect to provincial vicariates.* Provincial vicariates ought to be the first step toward founding a new "holy preaching," in a specific social and cultural context. This reinforcement of the intraprovincial link with the vicariates ought *to deepen everyone's awareness of the call to broaden the universality of the Order's mission and to give the audacity to open new missions.* From another point of view, Provinces are invited to reevaluate the distribution and composition of their communities so that *the witness of fraternal communion may always be part and parcel of the mission of evangelization.*

Another restructuring is at play in the evaluation of the centers for initial and specialized studies; they need to cooperate in identifying the benefits of collaboration and coordination on a regional basis. Along with this work, the more precise redefinition of the mission of the *Institutions that fall under the direct jurisdiction of the Master of the Order,* the reform of their governance structures, and the determination of their reciprocal relations with the provinces, ought to situate these institutions even more *in service to the mission of all*. A further restructuring has been begun and needs to be pursued in the area *of solidarity* among us, through establishing the office of solidarity (*Spem Miram Internationalis*). Further, an evaluation of the General Chapters, of their functioning in the life of the Order, of their preparation both at the level of the General Curia and at the level of the provinces, will seek to identify how they can better serve the life of the Order.

At the heart of this approach to reconfiguration, the ministry of preaching must of course hold a central place, That explains why in the perspective of this reorganization the chapter proposes to strengthen the dialogue among us about and from the preaching mission. This effort touches three principal areas: *Mission Forums* that will allow brothers working in the same apostolic field to dialogue among themselves and to reflect on the pastoral and theological dimensions of their mission; the *"Salamanca Process"* that is trying to promote theological and interdisciplinary dialogue concerning pastoral situations in particularly vulnerable contexts; and the exploitation of *apostolic creativity* in the "new continent" of the *Internet and the world of new social networks*. By focusing on these three areas, the chapter is calling all of us to strengthen our involvement in dialogue and in theological research at the heart of our ministry of preaching, giving a specific tone to our service in the church.

Such a dialogue should also give new opportunities for dialogue with contemporary knowledge, also with other religions and philosophies. It can also stimulate the contribution that our preaching of the Gospel will make to efforts to transform the world around us, an important dimension of "preaching to all the nations."

More generally, this reflection among the brothers concerning the ministry of preaching will certainly become the occasion to evaluate what we are already doing, to identify our need to enter new fields and find new means for evangelization, confronting human and social situations, cultures, new intellectual currents, and the search for meanings about things with which we regret to be too unfamiliar. Speaking of this "creativity" of evangelization, the chapter underlined the particular attention that we need to pay to promoting the *lay vocation to evangelization and, in this sense also, the priority to be given always to youth.*

So that is the demanding approach for which the Acts of this chapter has provided some orientations and that will lead us to the next General Chapter of 2016 in Bologna. The dearest wish of the capitulars was that this project should make it possible *that the act of thanksgiving in the celebration of the Jubilee will genuinely be a source for a renewed vigor for the future.*

In concluding this letter, I want to thank warmly the Province of Croatia and its Prior Provincial for having welcomed the chapter, as well as to thank Brother Mihael Mario Tolj, who performed the work of General Secretary so well, and also all the brothers who contributed in countless ways to the preparation, the communications work, and the celebration of this chapter. By the intercession of the Mother of God and of St. Dominic, may God give us in abundance the energy of the Spirit through whose inspiration we desire to be *"sent to preach the Gospel."*

Given at Rome at the Priory of Santa Sabina on the 28th of August in the year of Our Lord 2013, the Feast of Saint Augustine, Bishop and Doctor of the Church.

fr. Bruno Cadoré, o.p.
Maître de l'Ordre

fr. Franklin Buitrago Rojas, o.p.
a secretis

50/13/534 Trogi

5

UNDER
FR. BRUNO CADORE
MASTER OF THE ENTIRE ORDER OF PREACHERS

Former Masters of the Order
fr. **RADCLIFFE** Timothy
fr. **AZPIROZ COSTA** Carlos

Diffinitors

fr. **ALMARZA MEÑICA** Juan Manuel,. Province of Spain
fr. **LAFFAY** Augustin, Province of Tolouse
fr. **MALLEVRE** Michel, Province of France
fr. **GIORGIS** Roberto. Province of St. Dominic in Italy
fr. **CINELLI** Luciano, Province of Rome St. Catharine of Siena
fr. **BOVA** Damiano, Province of St. Thomas Aquinas in Italy.
fr. **SZABÓ** Bertalan, General Vicariate of Hungary
fr. **ZILS** Diethard, Province of Teutonia
fr. **OUNSWORTH** Richard, Province of England
fr. **PALUCH** Michał, Province of Poland
fr. **BOTELLA CUBELLS** Vicente, Province of Aragon
fr. **NÉMEC** Damián, Province of Bohemia
fr. **PETRIĆ** Perica Anastazio, Province of the Annuntiation of the B.V.M.
  in Croatia
fr. **CORREIRA FERNANDES** José Manuel, Province of Portugal
fr. **RODRIGUEZ FASSIO** Francisco José, Province of Betica
fr. **FRANSEN** Wijbe. Province of the Netherlands
fr. **NORTON** Gerard, Province of Ireland
fr. **RUBIO GUERRERO** Luis Javier, Province of St. James in Mexico
fr. **HERRERA HERRERA** Héctor, Province of St. John the Baptist in
  Peru.
fr. **GALEANO ROJAS** Guillermo Mauricio, Province of St. Louis Betrand
  in Colombia
fr. **DÁVILA YÁNEZ** Paúl Fernando, General Vicariate of St. Catharine of
  Siena in Ecuador
fr. **QUIJANO LEON** Francisco, General Vicariate of St. Laurence Martyr
  in Chile.
fr. **VILLASMIL BERMÚDEZ** Ángel Gabriel, Province of Our Lady of the
  Rosary

fr. **DE CALUWE** Mark, Province of St. Rose in Flanders

fr. **CÚNSULO** Rafael Roberto, Province of St Augustine Argentina

fr. **GARROTT** William Price, Province of St. Joseph in the U.S.A.

fr. **CILIA** Joseph, Province of St. Pius V, Malta

fr. **DIAS** Darren, Province of St. Dominic, Canada

fr. **THOMPSON** Augustine Craig, Province of the Most Holy Name in the U.S.A.

fr. **HELLMEIER** Paul Dominikus, Province of Upper Germany and Austria

fr. **SPAHN** James Anthony, Province of St. Albert the Great in the U.S.A.

fr. **FOOTE** Laurence Julian, Province of the Assumption of the B.V.M., Australia and New Zealand

fr. **TAVARES** André Luís, Province of fr. Bartholomew de las Casas in Brazil

fr. **SPICHTIG** Peter, Province of the Annuntiation of the B.V.M. in Switzerland

fr. **COLLIN** Dominique, General Vicariate of St. Thomas in Belgium

fr. **THAO DINH NGOC** Vincent, Province of the Queen of Martyrs in Vietnam

fr. **DE LA ROSA** Rolando, Province of the Philippines

fr. **SOLÓRZANO ZELAYA** Marcelo, Province of St. Martin de Porres in the U.S.A.

fr. **BHATTI** Rahmat, Vice Province of the Sons of Mary in Pakistan

fr. **VILLALOBOS RODRIGUEZ** Carlos Alberto, Vice Province of St. Vincent Ferrer in Central America

fr. **OGEDENGBE** Richard, Province of St. Joseph the Worker in Nigeria

fr. **SALDANHA** Navcen, Province of India

fr. **NDOLOMO BEMBU** Dominique, General Vicariate of the Republic of the Congo

fr. **MUYEBE** Stanislaus, General Vicariate of South Africa

fr. **PAN** Philip, General Vicariate of the Queen of China

fr. **SZPRĘGLEWSKI** Jacek, General Vicariate of the Most Holy Guardian Angels (Estonia, Latvia and Lithuania).

fr. **BALOG** Petro, General Vicariate of Russia and the Ukraine

fr. **SAMALOT RIVERA** Yamil, General Vicariate of the Holy Cross in Puerto Rico.

fr. **ŠAJDA** Česlav Peter, Province of Our Lady of the Rosary in Slovakia

fr. **KPONYO-HILLAH** Cyrille Ayayi, Vice Province of St. Augustine in West Africa fr. **CABALLERO SUARES** Yinmy, Vice Province of Bolivia

Delegates of the Vicariates

fr. **ABALOS ILLA** Roberto, Provincial Vicariate in Peru and Dominican Republic of the Province of Spain

fr. **BERNAL LLORENTE** Luis Carlos, Regional Vicariate in Central America of the Province of Aragon

fr. **MUTUKU** Dominic Wambua, Provincial Vicariate in East Africa of the Province of St. Joseph in the U.S.A.

Delegate of the Convents under the Immediate Jurisdiction of the Master of the Order
fr. **ADAM** Konštanc Miroslav

OTHER PARTICIPANTS AT THE GENERAL CHAPTER

Assistants of the Master of the Order and the Syndic of the Order

fr. **BOLAND** Vivian, Socius for the Provinces in Northern Europe and Canada and for Initial Formation; Vicar of the Master of the Order

fr. **DELIK** Wojciech, Socius for the Provinces in Central and Eastern Europe

fr. **MASCARI** Michael, Socius for the Intellectual Life

fr. **LOHALE** Prakash, Socius for the Apostolic Life

fr. **SAMBA** Gabriel, Socius for the Provinces of Africa

fr. **POSE** Javier, Socius for the Provinces of Latin America and the Caribbean

fr. **PROVECHO** Hilario, Syndic of the Order.

Brothers invited by the Master of the Order

fr. **SIGRIST** Marcel, Director of the EBAF

fr. **TUYEN** Joseph Mai Van

fr. **TROUT** Joseph

Invited by the Master of the Order from the Dominican Family

sr. **STRETTIOVA** Josefa, Monastery of Prague

sr. **BOHMER** Sara, Congregation of Sisters of the Third Order of Saint Dominic of Bethany

Mr. **BORNEWASSER** Klaus, Lay Fraternity of Las Casas, Dusseldorf

Moderators
fr. **O'CONNOR** John
fr. **SCAMPINI** Jorge
fr. **VAN LIER** Rick

Supporting Staff
fr. **TOLJ** Mihael Mario, Secretary General of the General Chapter
fr. **RAIC** Kristijan, Syndic of the General Chapter

Those Who Assisted in the Chapter

Interpreters
fr. **ALMAZAN** Leobardo
fr. **TORRES** Cristóbal
fr. **SANTIAGO** José
fr. **POQUILLON** Olivier
fr. **McSHANE** Philip
fr. **QUIJANO** Carlos
fr. **BAUZA SALINAS** Jean-Ariel
fr. **RIVERO** Manuel
fr. **LAROCHE** Victor
fr. **DUGAS** Julian
fr. **IZAGUIRRE** Carlos Ma
fr. **JABARES** Mario
fr. **MOISE** Junior Charles
fr. **MCCARTHY** Thomas
fr. **GARCIA BAUTISTA** Emilio
fr. **CROONENBERGHS** Didier
fr. **CASTRO** Sixto

Assistants
fr. **KORALIJA** Srecko, Cantor of the General Chapter
fr. **GAVRANOVIĆ** Ivan
fr. ILIČIĆ Ivan Dominik
fr. VLK Mirko Irenej
fr. DOKOZA Marko
fr. COTA Josip
fr. KAZOTTI Ante

fr. **KRŽELJ** Lovro
fr. **GAVRANOVIĆ** Anto
fr. **TOMIĆ** Ivan Marija
fr. **PAVLINOVIĆ** Marko
fr. **FOLNOVIĆ** Mladen

CHAPTER I: FORMALITIES

1. We report that with a circular letter, dated in Rome on November 21 of 2012, the Master of the Order, Fr. Bruno Cadoré, according to the norm of 413, II, convened the General Chapter of Diffinitors, to be held in the city of Trogir, Croatia, from July 22 to August 8, 2013.

2. We report that the Master of the Order, according to the norm of LCO 414, named fr. Mihael Mario Tolj as Secretary General of the Chapter on June 21, 2011.

3. We report that the Master of the Order, Fr. Bruno Cadoré invited to the General Chapter Diffinitors of Trogir, fr. Marcel Sigrist, Director of the Biblical School of Jerusalem, as well as fr. Joseph Mai Van Tuyen, cooperator brother of the Province of Vietnam and fr. Joseph Trout, cooperator brother of the Province of St. Albert the Great, U.S.A.

4. We report that the following members of the Dominican family attended as guests of the Master of the Order to the General Chapter of Diffinitors of Trogir: Sr. Josefa Strettiova, nun of the Monastery of Prague, Sr. Sarah Bohmer, sister of the Congregation of Dominican Sisters of Bethany, and Mr. Klaus Bornewasser, lay Dominican .

5. We report that on June 2, 2013 the Master of the Order, Fr. Bruno Cadoré, sent a letter to the Holy Father Francis, informing Him of the the General Chapter held in Trogir.

Rome, 2 June 2013

His Holiness
Pope Francis

Prot. 50/13/341 Trogir

Most Holy Father,

The Order of Preachers is preparing to celebrate its General Chapter (Chapter of Diffinitors) from 22 July to 8 August 2013 and I would like to ask you, with humility, to grant Your Apostolic Blessing to the brothers who will gather in Trogir (Croatia).

This chapter will mark the opening of the three-year period of preparation for the celebration eight-hundredth anniversary of the confirmation of the Order. This preparation, when the Church celebrates the Year of Faith and called for a renewal of evangelization, will be for the brothers, sisters and laity of the Order a favorable period to respond eagerly to this recall. The words and deeds of the Gospel with which You guide the Church from the beginning of Your ministry will be valuable guides for us in our determination to serve the Church, and supports the commitment that invites us to follow. I will be happy, later, to present to you the work of this Chapter .

During the Chapter, the World Youth Day will take place in Brazil and I assure You that we will be in communion with You at such an important moment in the life of the Church.

Thanking you in advance for Your blessing, I wish to express my thanks for Your ministry and assure You of my prayers and my respectful and fraternal greetings .

fr. Bruno Cadoré, OP
Master of the Order of Preachers

6. We report that on July 8 the Secretary of State of His Holiness Francis sent the following telegram to the Master of the Order and the Chapter:

Fr. Bruno Cadoré, OP,
General of the Order of Preachers

On the occasion of the General Chapter of Diffinitors of the Order of Preachers, held in Trogir, Croatia, in the context of the Year of Faith, the Holy Father Francis, grateful for the sentiments of filial loyalty to his Magisterium, sends to the participants his friendly good wishes, invoking the assistance of the Holy Spirit, and hopes that this important meeting will inspire renewed intentions of holiness and fidelity to the ideals of consecrated life for the building up of God's Kingdom in the generous service to the Church according to the specific charism of this order, following the shining example of the venerable Father St. Dominic and of all the saints of the Dominican Family .

His Holiness accompanies these wishes with a special remembrance in celebration of the Eucharist, and while asking you to pray for him, through the intercession of the Virgin Mary Queen of the Rosary, sends from his heart to you and your fellow chapter members the requested Apostolic Blessing, which I gladly extend to the entire Order.

Cardinal Tarcisio Bertone
Secretary of State of His Holiness

7.	We report that fr. Juan Manuel Almarza Meñica, fr. Luciano Cinelli and fr. James Spahn examined the testimonial letters of the vocals from the evening of July 21 to the morning of July 22,

8.	We report that fr. Peter Lalaiagalo, of the Province of the Assumption of the B.V.Mary of Australia and New Zealand, cannot participate in the Chapter due to difficulties in obtaining a visa.

9.	We report that the Master of the Order, Fr. Bruno Cadoré having heard the capitulars and according to the norm of LCO 417 § I, 3°, designated as reviewers of the text of the Acts of the Chapter for the Diffinitors: fr. Michel Mallèvre of the Province of France, fr. Richard Ounsworth of the Province of England and fr. Llorente Luis Carlos Bernal of the Regional Vicariate of the Province of Aragon in South America.

10.	We report that the General Chapter began on July 22, 2013 with a solemn Mass of the Holy Spirit, concelebrated by all the capiturlars and presided over by the Master of the Order, fr. Bruno Cadoré, whose homily invited the capitulars to follow the way of Mary Magdalen who was the Apostle of the Apostles, obeying the command of Jesus, "Go and tell my brothers...."

11.	We report that Monsignor Želimir Puljić, Archbishop de Zadar and President of the Episcopal Conference of Croatia, visited the capitulars on 22 July and offered a welcoming greeting.

12. We report that Mr. Ante Stipčić, mayor of the city of Trogir, paid a visit to the capitulars on July 22 to offer the welcome of the city.

13. We report that the Master of the Order, having consulted the capitulars, according to LCO 417 § I, 4°, confirmed the allocation, already prepared, of the members and of the presidents of the eight commissions.

Jubilee and Renewal of the Order - French

fr. LAFFAY Augustin – President
sr. BOHMER Sara
fr. BOTELLA CUBELLS Vicente
fr. DIAS Darren
fr. DINH Thao (Vincent)
fr. NDOLOMO BEMBU Dominique
fr. PETRIĆ Anastazio Perica
fr. RADCLIFFE Timothy
fr. SAMBA Gabriel
fr. SZPRĘGLEWSKI Jacek
fr. ZILS Diethard

Study - English

fr. NORTON Gerard – President
fr. COLLIN Dominique
fr. FOOTE Laurence Julian
fr. MASCARI Michael
fr. PALUCH Michał
fr. PAN Philip
 fr. ŠAJDA Česlav Peter
fr. SAMALOT RIVERA Yamil
fr. SIGRIST Marcel
fr. SPICHTIG Peter

Formation – Spanish/French

fr. VILLALOBOS RODRIGUEZ Carlos Alberto – President
fr. BOLAND Vivian
fr. GIORGIS Roberto
fr. KPONYO-HILLAH Cyrille Ayayi
fr. RODRIGUEZ FASSIO Francisco José
fr. RUBIO GUERRERO Luis Javier
fr. SPAHN James Anthony
fr. SZABÓ Bertalan
fr. TAVARES André Luís

Preaching - French/English

fr. QUIJANO LEON Francisco – President
fr. ABALOS ILLA Roberto
fr. ALMARZA MEÑICA Juan Manuel
fr. BHATTI Rahmat
Dnus BORNEWASSER Klaus
fr. CORREIA FERNANDES José Manuel
fr. BOVA Damiano
fr. LOHALE Prakash
fr. TUYEN MAI VAN Joseph
fr. OGEDENGBE Richard

Common Life – English/Spanish

fr. SALDANHA Naveen - President
fr. CABALLERO SUARES Yinmy
fr. CILIA Joseph
fr. CÚNSULO Rafael Roberto
fr. DELIK Wojciech
fr. FRANSEN Wijbe
fr. HERRERA HERRERA Héctor
fr. MUTUKU Dominic Wambua
fr. SOLÓRZANO ZELAYA Marcelo
sr. STRETTIOVA Josefa
fr. TROUT Joseph
fr. VILLASMIL BERMÚDEZ Ángel Gabriel

Government and Restructuring – French/English

fr. HELLMEIER Paul Dominikus – President
fr. BALOG Petro
fr. BERNAL LLORENTE Luis Carlos
fr. GARROTT William Price
fr. MALLEVRE Michel
fr. OUNSWORTH Richard
fr. POSE Javier

Economic Policy – Spanish/English

fr. DÁVILA YÁNEZ Paúl Fernando – President
fr. DE LA ROSA Rolando
fr. GALEANO ROJAS Guillermo Mauricio
fr. MUYEBE Stanislaus
fr. PROVECHO Hilario

LCO

fr. THOMPSON Augustine Craig – President
fr. ADAM Konštanc Miroslav
fr. AZPIROZ COSTA Carlos Alfonso
fr. CINELLI Luciano
fr. DE CALUWE Mark
fr. NĚMEC Damián

14. We report that the General Chapter approved as moderatiors for the plenary sessions: fr. John O'Connor of the Province of England, fr. Jorge Scampini of the Province of Argentina and fr. Rick Van Lier of the Province of Canada previously proposed by the Master of the Order.

15. We report that the Chapter approved the general rules of procedure proposed opportunely to the capitular friars.

16. We report that the Master of the Order, Fr. Bruno Cadoré presented his *Relatio de Statu Ordinis* to the Chapter, signed in Rome on February 22, 2013.

17. We report that the Socius of the Master of the Order, as well as the Syndic General and other official position of the Order shall present their respective reports which shall be placed at the disposition of the members of the Chapter.

18. We report that the the Master of the Order, fr. Bruno Cadoré, after the General Chapter of Rome in 2010, made the following appointments.

Vicar of the Master of the Order:
fr. Edward Ruane and, subsequently,
fr. Vivian Boland

Socii:
fr. Bernardino Prella, *Socius for the Provinces of the Iberian Peninsula*
fr. Vincent Lu, *Socius for the Provinces of Asia and the Pacific*
fr. Vivian Boland, *Socius for the Provinces of the Region of Northwest Europe   Socius for Initial Formation*
fr. Michael Mascari, *Socius for the Intellectual Life*
fr. Dominic Izzo, *Socius for the Provinces of the United States of America*

Procurator General of the Order
fr. Philippe Toxé

Syndic of the Order
fr. José Bernardo Vallejo and, subsequently,
fr. Hilario Provecho Álvarez

Secretary General:
fr. Franklin Buitrago Rojas

Vice-Secretary General and Secretary of the Master of the Order:
fr. Bonaventure Agbali

Promoters General:
fr. Eric Salobir, *Promoter General for Social Communications*
fr. Louis-Marie Ariño-Durand, *Promoter of the Rosary*

Other oficials:
fr. Olivier Poquillon: *Permanent Delegate to the United Nations*
fr. Bonaventure Agbali: *Director of I.D.I.*
fr. Dominic Izzo: *President of* Spem Miram *(Formerly: Director of Solidarity)*
fr. Wilmer Rojas Crespo: *Archivist of the Order*
fr. Michael Demkovich: *President of the International Dominican Foundation*
fr. Augustin Laffay: *Delegate for the promotion of the history of the O.P.*
fr. José Gabriel Mesa Angulo, *Chairman of the commission for the preparation of the program of the Jubilee of the Order which shall be presented and submitted for the approval of the General Chapter of Trogir (2013)*

19. We report that the Master of the Order issued the Decree of Canonical Erection of the Vice Province of Bolivia on October 25, 2012. That decree was read and entered into force on January 14, 2013.

20. We report that on January 13, 2012, the Master of the Order addressed to the whole Dominican Family the letter: *"Go and tell my brothers!": Dominicans and evangelization.*

21. We report that on May 31, 2012, Feast of the Visitation, the Master of the Order addressed to the whole Dominican family a letter about the celebration of the liturgy of the hours entitled: *"Laudare, Praedicare, Benedicere."*

22. We report that the Master of the Order, according to the norm of LCO 398 § III, made during this triennium numerous fraternal visits to different entities of the Order: France (22-Sep to 5-Oct-2010), Vicariate of Haiti and the Dominican Republic (12 to 17-Oct-2010), Freiburg Albertinum (1 to 4-Dec-2012), Freiburg Albertinum (1 to 3-Dec-2012), The Baltic States and Ukraine (14 to 23-Dec-2010), Asia-Pacific (17-Jan to 1-Feb-2011), Germany (16 to 23-Mar-2011), USA and Canada (1 to 21-Apr-2011), Pakistan (2 to 9-May-2011), Bologna (14 to 15-May-2011), North West Europe Region (5 to 20-Jun-2011), Spain (24 to 28-Jun-2011), Latin America and

Caribbean Region (1 to 16-Jul-2011), Africa Region (1 to 21-Aug-2011), U.S. Province of St. Martin (22 to 26-Oct-2011), Palermo (5 to 6-Nov-2011), Spain (20 to 29-Dec-2011), Abidjan (20 to 23-Jul-2012), Lima (12 to 14-Aug-2012), Spain (17 to 19-Sep-2012), Bari (5- to 6-Dec-2012), Mexico (25 to 31-Jan-2013), Slovakia (17 to 19-May-2013).

23. Canonical Visitations were also made to: Croatia (22 to 30-Sep-2011), Province of the Most Holy Name of Jesus–USA (10 to 21-Oct-2011), Mexico (6 to 19-Dec-2011), South Belgium (8 to 12-Jan-2012), Congo (17 to 31-Jan-2012), Upper Germany and Austria (7 to 17-Feb-2012), Tolouse (7 to 18-Mar-2012), Convento San Stephen of Jerusalem (2 to 8-Apr-2012), Poland (15 Apr to 10-May-2012), Baltic Lands (3 to 7-Jun-2012), Russia–Ukraine (8 to 12-Jun-2012), Colombia (15 to 30-Jun-2012), U.S. Province of St. Martin (1 to 18-Jul-2012), Ecuador (17 to 22-Aug-2012), Canada (23 to 31-Aug-2012), Puerto Rico (25 to 27-Sep-2012), Venezuela (30-Sep to 3-Oct-2012), Central America (4 to 16-Nov-2012), Philippines (7 to 21-Dec-2012), Portugal (3 to 9-Jan-2013), Netherlands (12 to 18-Jan-2013), Flanders (18 to 24-Jan-2013), Santo Domingo, Haiti and Cuba (25 Mar to 7-Apr-2013), Hungary (16 to 19-Mar-2013), Russia–Ukraine (20 to 26-Mar-2013), Holy Rosary (7 to 8-May-2013), Australia (6 to 22-Jun-2013), Chile (23 to 26-Jun-2013), Argentina (27 Jun to 5-Jul-2013), Vicariate of Aragon in South America (6 to 9-Jul-2013).

24. We report that on June 3, 2012 our brother fr. Jean-Joseph Lataste, founder of the Dominican Sisters of Bethany was beatified.

25. We report that on October 13, 2012 our brothers fr. Joaquin Gonzalez Raymond Brown and fr. José María González Solís, martyred during religious persecution in Spain were beatified.

26. We report that on May 12, 2013 our brother fr. Alejandro Longo was canonized with the group of martyrs of Otranto (Italy).

27. We report that His Holiness Pope Benedict XVI received in private audience the Master of the Order, Fr. Bruno Cadoré, on March 11, 2011.

28. We report that the Master of the Order, Fr. Bruno Cadoré, participated in the XIII General Assembly of the Synod of Bishops, held in Rome from October 7 to 28, 2012.

29. We report that His Holiness Pope Benedict XVI created Archbishop Dominik Duka, OP, Archbishop of Prague, a Cardinal of the Holy Roman Church.

30. We report that His Holiness Pope Benedict XVI appointed Archbishop Joseph Augustine Di Noia, OP, Titular Archbishop of Oregon City, as Vice President of the Pontifical Commission "Ecclesia Dei".

31. We report that His Holiness Pope Benedict XVI appointed Archbishop Jean-Louis Bruguès, OP, Archbishop Emeritus of Angers, as archivist and librarian of the Holy Roman Church.

32. We report that during the last three years, the Holy Father has appointed as bishops: fr. Omar Alberto Sánchez Cubillos of the Province of Colombia who was named bishop of Tibú (Colombia), fr. Charles Morerod of the Province of Switzerland who was named bishop of Lausanne, Geneva and Fribourg (Switzerland) and fr. Jean-Paul Vesco of the Province of France who was named bishop of Oran (Algeria).

33. We report that fr. Serge Thomas Bonino was appointed Secretary General of the International Theological Commission.

34. We report that since the last General Chapter held in Rome, the Master of the Order has been promoted to the degree of Master of Sacred Theology: fr. Paul Murray of the Irish Province, Fr. Louis Roy of the Province of Canada, fr. Alberto Escallada Tijero and fr. Celada Gregorio Luengo of the Province of Spain, fr. Gilles Emery of the Province of Switzerland; fr. Jean-Luc Vesco, fr. Benoit-Dominique de La Soujeole, fr. Serge Thomas Bonino and fr. Jean-Michel Maldamé of the Province of

Toulouse; fr. Albino Barrera, fr. Terence Stephen Keegan and fr. Michel Romanus Cessario of the Province of St. Joseph in the U.S.A.

35. We report that during the days of October 31 to November 3, 2012, as part of the celebration of the 50th anniversary of the canonization of St. Martin de Porres in Lima (Perú) an international meeting was held involving cooperator brothers from all regions of the Order.

36. We report that the Master of the Order participated in the celebrations of the centenary of the Province of Canada (1911-2011), the 50th anniversary of the presence of the Order in Ivory Coast (1962-2012) and the 50th anniversary of the restoration of the Province of Portugal (1962-2012). He also participated in the celebration of the fourth centenary of the Pontifical and Royal University of Santo Tomas in Manila (1611-2011).

37. We report that the Master of the Order participated the Assembly of the International Dominican Youth Movement held from July 7 to July 15, 2013 in the city of Bogotá (Columbia).

38. We report that on August 3, the feast of Blessed Augustine Kazotic, the Chapter celebrated the Eucharist in Trogir, his hometown, in front of the convent church. The celebration was presided by Cardinal Josip Bozanic, Archbishop of Zagreb, who was responsible for the homily. Also participating were Bishop Marin Barišić, Archbishop of Split-Makarska, Bishop Ante Ivas, Bishop of Šivenik, and Fray Anto Gravić, Prior Provincial. and many faithful .

39. We report that the General Chapter concluded its work on the 8th of August, the Solemnity of Our Holy Father Dominic, with a solemn concelebrated Mass in the Dominican church of St. Catherine of Alexandria in the city of Split. The Eucharist was presided by Archbishop Marin Barišić, Archbishop of Split-Makarska. The sermon was given by fr. Bruno Cadoré, Master

of the Order. During the same celebration fr. Kristijan Dominik Gerbic made his solemn profession and fr. Ivan Gavranović and fr. Joseph Trout renewed their simple professions.

CHAPTER II: PROEMIUM

Sent to Preach the Gospel

40.   In 2016, we will celebrate the eighth centenary of the confirmation of the Order by Pope Honorius III. A Jubilee for the people of Israel was a time of joy and renewal when "you shall return, every one of you, to your property and every one of you to your family" (Lev 25:10). If our Jubilee invites us to return to the origins of the Order, paradoxically it is so that we will remember how St. Dominic sent out his first friars from their house, their family, and their nation so as to discover the joy and freedom of itinerancy. Our mobility means more than moving from one place to another. As disciples of Christ, we are sent to preach the Gospel. By sharing the life of the One who, sent by the Father, breathes out his Spirit upon us, we acquire the interior freedom that alone makes us attentive to the appeals of our human sisters and brothers.

The Charism of Preaching

41.   In celebrating eight centuries of existence, we are invited more than ever to *laudare, benedicere et praedicare*. It is above all God whom we praise for the grace that he gave to Dominic, whose charism of preaching continues to be expressed in and for the world, *in medio Ecclesiae*. This ministry of preaching that we share with the whole church is still vital and urgent today so that the Gospel may ring out from one end of the world to the other. So this anniversary gives us the occasion to look towards the future, confident in the promises of God who "did not send the Son into the world to condemn the world, but in order that the world might be saved through him" (Jn 3:17). Looking to the future, we recognize that we have a lot to learn still about our history, about its moments of shadow and its moments of light, and about the brothers and sisters who went before us among whom were many authentic witnesses to the Kingdom. Our history is a school of truth and humility. It is the source of renewal and hope for the mission of Preachers.

Preaching the Word of God

42. Preaching means making the mystery of the Incarnation present to men and women today. "The Word became flesh" to teach us the Truth of God and the truth about our humanity. To fulfill this service of the Word well, like St. Dominic, we have to be seekers of the Truth rooted in the life of Christ. The renewal of our Dominican life begins with the unification of our whole existence through attentive listening to the Word—a life of prayer and contemplation in silence and study. The foundation of our Dominican formation is acquiring a human, spiritual and relational maturity that can bear witness to how the Word of God makes people more fully human and makes our communities of brothers capable of expressing the friendship that God wants to exist among us.

The Demands of Preaching

43. Preparation for our Jubilee also implies a dimension of *metanoia* or conversion, because our communal and individual lives are shaped by the lifestyles and the opinions around us that we somehow absorb: nihilism, superficiality, addictions and consumerism in the surrounding world, forms of relativism and fundamentalism, a passion to possess, to have power and to look good. All this can infect our Dominican life with individualism and with a bourgeois spirit, with a loss of strength and of the credibility necessary for proclaiming the gospel. More than ever, we need to remember that "faith without works is dead" (James 2:17) and as preachers of grace, we have to show by word and example how faith transforms human existence; renews the heart, the spirit, and the body; and how the social realities of the world are called to become signs of the coming of the Kingdom.

The Fruitfulness of Study

44. As we know, St. Dominic sent the friars to study in the universities and to be formed there in contact with the new sciences. Today, more than ever, the complexity of the human condition and the major changes that affect people's lives invite us to seek to understand the world in which we live that

"God loved so much" (John 3:16). Today St. Dominic would send his brothers and sisters to be right in the middle of these transformations so that they could address the questions being posed there and enter into dialogue with those seeking to build a more human world. Nourished by our own traditions, we will be able to bear humble service to the Word of truth, to show how theology is no stranger to any of these contemporary questions, and to offer a biblical and Christian vision of humanity, of human dignity, and of the incommensurable value of what is truly human. For us, study is not just a stage in formation but a way of being: it nourishes our whole life and makes it fruitful. Nourished by the Word of God that we must learn to listen to, read, meditate, and study with renewed vigor, we will be able to address the questions of our world that are really just so many new opportunities for Friars Preachers. Indeed our Jubilee gives us the occasion to consider creatively, in cooperation with the nuns, the sisters, and the lay members of the Order, the ways of consecrating ourselves anew to study for the sake of preaching.

A Style of Life

45. Our style of life flows from this personal and communal balancing of study, contemplation, and liturgical prayer, each element enlivening the others. The genius of our founder was to give us flexible, democratic structures of government so that the Order would be able to devote itself entirely to evangelization and address the joys and sorrows, the hopes and fears of people of every age. Our constitutions are a source of liberation, not constraint. Continually modified and renewed in the light of new needs, the constitutions find their basis and their inspiration in the following of Christ. Our laws remind us that Dominican life is lived in community. Their full meaning is seen in their concrete application to our search for fraternal communion, as in the sharing of our goods and of our gifts. St. Albert the Great wrote in this vein: *in dulcedine societatis, quaerere veritatem* ("in the joy of fraternity, pursue the truth"). Indeed, the pleasure of our fraternal life, and the joy and the forgiveness that we share with one another will constitute our best evangelization in this world wracked with violence, conflict and intolerance. Weren't our first com-munities called "the holy preaching"?

An Order in Evolution

46. This explains why our Order has been caught up since the General Chapter of Rome in a process of renewal and of structural transformation for the sake of strengthening our preaching mission. This administrative restructuring is not being done for its own sake or to abandon our presence in certain locations. It seeks rather to discern carefully the appropriate structures that will restore the dynamism of our Order in all of its parts and will respond better to the call that St. Dominic himself gave to the first friars "to preach, to study, and to found priories."

An Apostolic Life

47. Consequently, the charism that we received from St. Dominic that entrusts us with the task of preaching, since confirmed by the church, requires us to live in the way the apostles lived, "giving testimony to the resurrection of the Lord Jesus" (Acts 4:33). More than ever, it is by devoting ourselves "to the apostles' teaching and fellowship, to the breaking of bread and the prayers" (Acts 2:42) that we will be faithful to the prophetic vision of St. Dominic, who wanted an Order entirely consecrated to the preaching of the Word.

Good News for Everybody

48. Sent by Christ "to bring good news to the poor" (Lk 4:18), we are called to enter into the concrete conditions of men and women today in order to share with them a word of hope and of friendship, above all in these times when so many have lost hope for a more human world. Today many people are affected by the results of the worldwide economic, social and moral crisis causing so much vulnerability and intolerance. Our preaching will demonstrate our compassion for those who suffer, bear witness to our solidarity with the socially rejected and with those who live on the fringes of our societies, and speak prophetically to denounce whatever is dehumanizing, above all calling people to a change of mind and heart. Others suffer from social pressures that foster fundamentalism, violence and persecution. Our preaching will be on the lookout for any kind of possible dialogue; it will aim to promote respectful listening to others and ways of speaking that are not confrontational but that humbly seek the truth along with them. Finally, in the context of secularization, our preaching will aim to show how faith gives meaning to life, integrates the person, and puts us in relation to God and to others. Faith opens up an unexpected horizon of human freedom.

"Go to My Brothers and Speak to Them" (Jn 20:17)

49. Celebrating eight centuries of the existence of the Order of Preachers will consist less in commemorating an anniversary than in pushing forward, all of us together enthusiastically, towards the future of our charism. We are confident that the ministry of evangelization will remain a necessity for the church at the service of the world. Indeed, "How beautiful are the feel of those who proclaim peace and who bring good news!" (Rm 10:15) We believe that God has a magnificent plan for the whole human community and that he has chosen us, despite our weaknesses, to be joyful witnesses to his good news.

CHAPTER III: THE JUBILEE AND THE RENEWAL
OF THE MISSION OF EVANGELIZATION OF THE ORDER

Opening of the Jubilee

50. *[Declaration]* We declare that the Order will celebrate a Jubilee Year with the theme "Sent to preach the Gospel." This marks the issuing of the Bulls promulgated by Pope Honorius III eight centuries ago, confirming the foundation of the Order, in 1216 and 1217.

51. *[Declaration]* We declare that in celebrating a Jubilee the Order seeks to renew itself by entering into a dynamic process that culminates in sending the friars to preach anew, just as Dominic sent the first brethren. In preparing for the Jubilee we affirm that as Dominicans we are sent to preach the Good News of the Resurrection of Christ. As we prepare to be sent anew we ask ourselves: By whom are we sent? To whom are we sent? With whom are we sent? What do we bring with us in being sent?

   We are conscious that we will share the joy and the freedom of being sent, following Saint Dominic, with the whole Dominican Family.

52. *[Thanksgiving]* We thank fr. José Gabriel Mesa and the members of the working team who prepared the Jubilee proposal.

53. *[Ordination]* We ordain the Master of the Order to name a Coordinator and Steering Committee as soon as possible to oversee the Jubilee and to work together with the Provincial Promoters of the Jubilee.

54. *[Ordination]* We ordain the priors provincials who have not already done so to appoint a provincial promoter of the Jubilee and inform the General Curia before 22 December 2013.

Our History

55.   *[Declaration]* As brothers and sisters in the Order of Preachers, we inherit a common history that is both rich and complex and that impels us to proclaim the Gospel through apostolic preaching—the *missio ad gentes*. This history still continues to shape the members of the Dominican family today. The Order has given much to humanity on all the continents of the world: understanding of the faith, philosophical research, promotion of and reflection on human rights, works of art, scientific writing, works of charity, and much else.

However, the members of the Order have often been unequal to their mission. We ought to have the courage to examine the shadowy or dubious dimensions of our history. For example, the four scholarly colloquia organized by the Instituto Storico Ordinis Praedicatorum (ISOP) on the involvement of the Dominicans in the Inquisition gave evidence of our desire to make clear our involvement in this history so that it will be available to coming generations.

56.   *[Recommendation]* In the light of this, we recommend to those promoting the Jubliee:

1. to make sure that historical sources concerning St. Dominic and the birth of the Order are available in scholarly editions;

2. to strive to make known the witness to holiness of the Dominican Order in all of its dimensions;

3. to promote knowledge of the artistic and spiritual patrimony of the Order;

4. to study the history of preaching;

5. to encourage the use of information technology for sharing data about this history in order to permit a communication of our resources on a worldwide scale.

The promoters of the Jubilee ought to be helped by their superiors and by the Regents of Studies.

Criteria for the Celebration of the Jubliee

57. *[Commission]* We commission the steering committee for the Jubilee for the whole Order and the provincial promoters of the Jubilee to prepare their programs in conformity with the following criteria:

1. The celebration of the Jubilee over the next three years means entering into a dynamic process of renewal (mission, spiritual life, common life, institutions) and not just the celebration of events.

2. The celebration should not be self-referential but oriented towards God, from whom we receive the gift of our Dominican vocation, and towards those to whom we are sent.

3. Remembering our history is not for self-glorification but to remind us of our origins in a spirit of gratitude, and to help us to discover the place of itinerancy in our way of life.

4. The celebration of the Jubilee is an opportunity for us, in an ecumenical spirit, to venture into "new worlds" in dialogue and solidarity with the forgotten, the poor, the victims of violence and oppression. We should reach out to believers of other religious traditions and non-believers alike, close to them in their search for meaning.

5. The celebration of the Jubilee should reflect the creativity that is needed to preach today through the arts (poetry, painting, film, etc.) and modem means of communication (internet, YouTube, Twitter, etc.).

6. The events that celebrate the Jubilee are most powerful when they have symbolic value like Pope Francis' first journey outside Rome to the margins of Europe to the people and refugees of Lampedusa.

7. In choosing sites for the celebration of the Jubilee new foundations where the order is being born should be privileged.

8. Resources (intellectual and economic) and materials (art, audio-visual, print) for the celebration of the Jubilee should be shared.

9. We must take care to include all branches of the Dominican Family in the celebration.

10. The celebration of the Jubilee must try to capture the voice and imagination of the young and to lead them to participate in our mission of evangelization.

Calendar and Proposals for the Jubilee

58. *[Recommendation]* Marking the time of the Jubilee.
1. Between 2006 and 2016, each year is dedicated in the Order to a special theme. The General Chapter recommends to the steering committee for the Jubilee to take these themes into account.

2. We ask the steering committee for the Jubilee to take into account the events being prepared in the French Provinces to commemorate in 2015 the opening of the little community around St. Dominic in the Maison Pierre Seilhan in Toulouse in the spring of 1215.

3. The Jubilee Year properly speaking will be celebrated between November 7, 2015 (Feast of All Saints of the Order) and January 21, 2017 (the date of the Bull *Gratiarum omnium largitori* of Pope Honorius III).

59. *[Recommendation]* Places for Celebrating the Jubilee
We recommend to the steering committee for the Jubilee to give privileged attention to the following places in celebrating the events of the Jubilee:

31

1. places linked to the life of St. Dominic and to the birth of the Order of Preachers; in particular, Calaruega, Palencia, Osma, Fanjeaux, Prouille, Toulouse, Rome and Bologna;

2. places where members of the Order are specially consecrated to prayer and the contemplative life: monasteries and shrines;

3. places on the frontiers of humanity (cf. General Chapter of Avila), "places where human community is breaking down" (cf. Pierre Claverie), places where the Order is in the process of growing.

The Program for the Jubilee

60. *[Commission]* Publication of a program
We commission the steering committee for the Jubilee to publish a booklet/program in Spanish, French and English before the end of the year 2014.

This booklet/program will include especially the following points:

1. an explanation of the theme and the meaning of the Jubilee in conformity with the spirit described in the Acts of this chapter.

2. an historical sketch describing the principal stages in the birth of the Order and the elements for a biography of St. Dominic, taking recent historical research into account.

3. a calendar of celebrations and events organized for the occasion of the Jubilee at the level of the whole Order, as well as a presentation of the principal events organized in the Provinces, the regions of the Order, and by institutions related to the Order.

61. *[Petition]* We petition the steering committee to include the following elements in the program prepared at the level of the universal Order:

1. an assembly of the International Dominican Youth Movement (IDYM) linked to the World Youth Day scheduled for Kraków in 2016;

2. an exhibition presenting the works of contemporary Dominican artists in a well-known public site (an airport terminal, for example);

3. an exhibition on movable panels presenting the life of St. Dominic, his mission, and the birth of the Order; this exhibition should be prepared in such a way that it can be translated into different languages and duplicated so as to be at the disposal of the Provinces and of the whole Dominican family;

4. a collaboration with members of the Dominican family who are competent and active in information technology for preaching the Gospel through the Internet;

5. a coordination among the different communities on the route of St. Dominic's many journeys, from Calaruega to Bologna, in order to assist pilgrims on their way and to help them discover the life of St. Dominic at its roots;

6. a symposium, organized cooperatively by the institutions under the immediate jurisdiction of the Master of the Order, addressing the proclamation of the Gospel and its ecumenical challenges in the context of secularization and the expansion of new religious movements;

7. in the context of the Salamanca Process, an event consecrated to the heritage of Vitoria and to the implications of his thought for the challenges posed by human rights today (the situation of migrants, refugees, indigenous peoples...);

8. a pilgrimage of student brothers representing all the Provinces of the Order with the Master of the Order;

9. a meeting with the pope so that the Order may renew its Dominican mission at the heart of the church.

62. *[Recommendation]* Other colloquia and events

We recommend to the Master of the Order and to Prior Provincials responsible for the brothers of their Provinces undertaking and preparing scholarly projects, that they should contribute to the dialogue of the Gospel with the contemporary world in these ways:

1. critical editions of historical texts concerning the Order;

2. the development and exposition of the Bible in its traditions (BEST), the project of the École Biblique et Archéologique Française de Jérusalem (EBAF);

3. theological colloquia (such as The Order of Preachers and Vatican II, Toronto, 2015; the Third Thomistic Symposium, Toulouse, 2016; etc.);

4. a colloquium on the Word of God organized in collaboration with the Angelicum, the Biblical School of Jerusalem, and the postulators for the cause of Père Lagrange.

We encourage these centers of research of the Order to develop projects in the context of the Jubilee and to make them known to the Order through the steering committee for the Jubilee.

CHAPTER IV: THE FOLLOWING OF CHRIST

United in Faith

63. *[Exhortation]* We exhort the brothers to rediscover the richness of our liturgical life in common as an essential part of our Dominican life (cf. LCO 63). Each community should celebrate the liturgy as an expression of living faith and an act of preaching, taking into account the following criteria:

1. The celebration of the liturgy is an expression of the life of the Church and the unity of the brothers. The mere fulfilment of rubrics does not of itself assure this truth.

2. Our liturgical celebration must take root in the ongoing liturgical tradition of the Church, and of the Order and its own elements, taking into account the criteria for the renovation of the liturgy from Vatican II, subsequent directives from the Congregation for Divine Worship and the Discipline of the Sacraments, and the directions of the International Commission for the Liturgy of the Order (ACG 2010 Rome 75).

3. Our Constitutions remind us that the Conventual Mass is the clearest sign of our unity in the Church and in the Order; therefore "it is preferable that the Conventual Mass be concelebrated" by the priestly brothers (LCO 59 § II).

4. Preaching should be included in the Conventual Mass or other liturgical celebrations to foster the sharing of our faith.

64. *[Petition]* We petition all Provinces and Vicariates to inform the President of the International Liturgical Commission of the Order on what progress they have made in the translation of the *Proprium Ordinis Praedicatorum* (ACG 2010 Rome 75 §§ 1-3), and to report even if no progress has been made.

65. *[Exhortation]* Our personal prayer is rooted in common prayer and our common prayer in personal prayer. We exhort all the brothers to keep in mind the value of individual and prayerful reading of the Word of God (cf. LCO 66 § I), keeping in mind the motto of the Order *contemplata aliis tradere* and not forgetting that "*aliis*" means first of all our own brothers in community.

66. *[Commendation]* In order to provide for spaces of renewal and healing for our fraternal relations, we recommend that all communities include at least once a year a time of communal reconciliation among the brothers (ACG 2010 Rome 62 § 5; ACG 2007 Bogotá 192; ACG 2004 Kraków 221).

67. *[Petition]* From the example of the life of the apostles found in the Scriptures, St. Augustine says that "the chief motivation for your sharing life together is to live harmoniously in the house and to have one heart and one soul seeking God" (*Rule of St. Augustine* chapter 1). The contemporary thrust to polarization in political, social, cultural, economic and many other spheres presents a challenge to our commitment to this apostolic life. We petition all communities in the Order to dedicate a regular chapter meeting within the next six months to revising their life in common in view of our call to be of one heart and soul against this present ill of polarization. In particular the following questions should be considered:

1. Does the present practice in the community seek the common good, or does it mirror the pursuit of political parties to prove themselves right and their contraries wrong for the sake of gaining office?

2. In our community deliberations, do we often make use of our procedure in order to exclude our competitors rather than to let our decisions be the result of a search for the common wisdom and the seeking out of mutual understanding?

3. Do we seek in our communities to enter into mutual understanding through dialogue with open hearts and a firm commitment to understand and consider one another, or do we manipulate the structures to get what one group of brothers thinks is right?

68. *[Commission]* We commission the Master of the Order to have St. Francisco Coll y Guitart, O.P. inserted into the Liturgical Calendar of the Order on May 19, with the rank of obligatory memorial, and to have St. Zdislava of Lemberk inserted into the

Liturgical Calendar of the Order, insofar as this has not been done, on January 4, with the rank of obligatory memorial. This legislation does not prevent Provinces from requesting permission to celebrate these saints on other days, should their celebration be impeded by a local saint.

Mission as Community

69. *[Petition]* We petition the Master of the Order to write a letter on the subject of the community project.

70. *[Petition]* We petition all brothers to take heed of the need for their active and responsible participation in the building of our life in common by integrating individual apostolic initiatives into the framework of their community project.

71. *[Exhortation]* Our vows ask us to go beyond the natural instinct for self-preservation and continually follow the command of Christ to "go, sell all you have ... then come, follow me" (Matthew 19:21). In this spirit, we exhort all brothers who are leading our initiatives in ministry always to remember that they use their gifts and talents for the common mission of the Order.

72. *[Exhortation]* We exhort Priors Provincial to ensure that provincial ministerial commitments be structured and exe- cuted so that, while they may depend on the personality and gifts of some particular friar, they can be handed over graciously when appropriate.

73. *[Commendation]* In order to foster the greatest participation of brothers in common life, we recommend that all communities, in their development of the community project, take special care to respect the needs of the ministries of the brothers when scheduling liturgy, chapters and other community functions. In the same way individual brothers should always consider their responsibilities to common life when scheduling their ministries.

74. *[Exhortation]* In order to favor the participation of all of our friars in common life, we exhort all Provincials and Vicars Provincial to consider whether they should restructure their presence in their territories with a view to enabling brothers who live alone, or in smaller communities in proximity to one another, to move into larger communities or convents.

75. *[Ordination]* We ordain that all Priors Provincial and Vicars Provincial, with their respective councils, and in accordance with LCO 32 § II, establish and implement norms to be followed in regard to those friars who repeatedly refuse to hand over their income to the community in spite of fraternal correction (cf. ACG 2004 Kraków 238).

76. *[Ordination]* We ordain that all Priors Provincial and Vicars Provincial review every year the situation of brothers who have been outside community for long periods of time, taking into account the Constitutions of the Order and Canon Law.

Care for Our Vulnerable

77. *[Exhortation]* We exhort all Provinces, Vice Provinces and Vicariates to develop policies and seek to procure sufficient means to tend to, accompany and care for elderly and sick brothers. Beside professional accompaniment, the spiritual and fraternal presence of the brothers to them must not be lacking (ACG 2007 Bogotá 173-175).

78. *[Petition]* We petition all communities to take into account in their community project those elderly brothers who have the capacity to remain at least partially active in the ministry of preaching and teaching, and to value the wisdom they bring from a life of experience in the preaching mission of the Order.

79. *[Ordination]* We ordain that all Provinces, at their next Chapter, verify that their policies are in accordance with ACG 2004 Kraków 232-236, ACG 2007 Bogotá 181-184 and ACG 2010 Rome 71 regarding the questions of the affective health and addictions of the Brothers.

Cooperator Brothers

80. *[Declaration]* We declare that the identity of the Order as a "clerical order" (*The Fundamental Constitution* § VI) does not imply that all its members are clerics. The contemporary promotion of the Cooperator Brother vocation is an opportunity to break down all forms of clericalism contrary to our fraternal life, rather than to clericalise the Cooperator Brother vocation.

81. *[Thanksgiving]* We commend all brothers involved in the "Dominican Cooperator Brother Study" for their commitment to rejuvenating this vital vocation in the Order.

82. *[Exhortation]* We exhort Priors to encourage and support the communal reflection of the final report produced by the "Dominican Cooperator Brother Study" (cf. *Relatio de Statu Ordinis* of the Master of the Order, 2013: 113).

CHAPTER V: STUDY

All Friars

83. *[Exhortation]* We exhort all friars to mark this time of jubilee by renewing their study of the life-giving Word of God, remembering particularly the Gospel of St. Matthew and the Letters of St. Paul.

84. *[Exhortation]* We exhort each local community and each friar to take time to prepare a program of study linked to their ministry of salvation (cf. LCO 76) in the context of the Jubilee.

Provincial Centers of Studies

85. *[Commission]* We commission all the Regents of Studies and the superiors of Provinces and Vicariates in each region to meet together at least once before the General Chapter of 2016 in order to study, and implement where possible, the kinds of concrete collaboration needed in that region. Keeping in mind LCO 91, this may entail the amalgamation of centers, as well as the diversification of academic courses and programs amongst the centers of study and other Dominican academic institutes in the region, including online and distance learning, and perhaps other measures (cf. ACG 2010 Rome: 89-92). This reconfiguration of our centers of study should foster the foundation of centers for specialized studies and research within the regions where there are none, enriching with the diverse cultural perspectives of the Order the intellectual contribution expected of us by the Church and society. This process is expected also to provide for a better distribution of our human, library, financial, building, and administrative resources, a better student enrollment and, most of all, a focused objective of each Dominican center of studies.

86. *[Commission]* We commission the Permanent Commission for the Promotion of Studies in the Order to facilitate and supervise this process, based on what was ordained to that Commission by the Chapter of Rome 2010 (ACG 2010 Rome: 97; 100). A report of this process of regional reconfiguration of our centers of study must be presented to the Socius for Intellectual Life, in time for him to prepare his own report for the 2016 General Chapter.

87.   *[Petition]* We ask the Socius for Intellectual Life to keep the regents and the provincials informed about the work of the Permanent Commission for the Promotion of Studies. We ask him to organize a virtual network that will allow all the regents of the Order to keep in touch and to develop common projects.

88.   *[Ordination]* We ordain that provincial centers of study make comprehensive academic documentation available to their provincials, provincial councils, and the provincial commissions for intellectual life when requested to do so. Where appropriate, these should include independent reports by peer academics in comparable institutions, and clarification of any relationships entered into with accrediting bodies.

89.   *[Petition]* We petition the Master of the Order, in his visitation of entities where a Provincial Center of Studies has been established (cf. LCO 91-2), to ensure that appropriate and adequate procedures of academic appraisal have been set in place in relation to such centers.

90.   *[Commendation]* We recommend that, in the task of renewing our study life and mission, the Socius for Intellectual Life, the Regents of Studies, Moderators and Conventual Lectors take into account the participation of members of all the branches of the Dominican family, including in teaching, research and administration. Their contribution is especially important in our provincial centers of study and in the institutions under the immediate jurisdiction of the Master of the Order.

91.   *[Ordination]* We ordain that all Provinces and Vicariates that do not have Dominican Centers of initial formation make sure to provide for all their students in formation the necessary supplementary education in relation to the spiritual, philosophical and theological heritage of the Order.

92. *[Ordination]* We ordain that, before the General Chapter of 2016, each Province prepare a new or revised program of studies for cooperator brothers, taking into account the forthcoming final report of the "Dominican Cooperator Brothers Study," the diversity of ministries of the cooperator brothers, and the vision articulated by the Second Vatican Council (cf. *Perfectae Caritatis* 18).

93. *[Commission]* We commission the Master of the Order to incorporate a program of studies for the cooperator brothers into the coming revision of the *Ratio Studiorum Generalis* (cf. ACG 2010 Rome: 100.3).

94. *[Exhortation]* Recognizing that scientific research is an important part of the culture of study in our Order, we exhort Provincials and Regents of Studies to support gifted brothers who wish to pursue scientific specialization and dedicate themselves to research. Specialization and research in areas other than theology are to be encouraged. Brothers working in research are called to use their expertise to enrich the life of study in the Order. They are also invited to make use of their specialized knowledge in appropriate forms of their apostolate.

95. *[Petition]* We ask the different centers of study in the Order to take into account the new forms of digital media, especially in their theological and philosophical studies, in collaboration with the General Promoter of Social Communications and the OPTIC network (Order of Preachers for Technology, Information and Communication).

96. *[Exhortation]* Given the importance of the transformations taking place in the religious landscape, we exhort Provincials and Regents of Studies to support the study of ecumenical and interreligious dialogues in their entities, and to form brothers specialized in this field. (cf. *Ratio Studiorum Generalis* 21)

Academic Institutions under the Master of the Order

97. *[Thanksgiving]* We wish to thank the brothers that serve in the École Biblique et Archéologique Française, the theological faculty at Fribourg University, the Historical Institute, the Leonine Commission, and the Pontifical University of St Thomas ("Angelicum") in Rome. We are glad to recognize their important theological contribution to the intellectual life of the Order, the Church, and the world.

Recruitment of New Professors

98. *[Commendation]* The houses and institutions under the immediate jurisdiction of the Master of the Order all face the same structural problem in finding new professors, not being the responsibility of specific Provinces. Because the Order values the work of these institutions, we strongly recommend that Superiors and Regents of Studies encourage the intellectual specialization of any gifted student, especially in academic fields where these institutions have been successfully working for the mission of the Order and the Church.

99. *[Petition]* We ask that each of the institutions under the immediate jurisdiction of the Master of the Order build relationships with the Provinces including closer collaboration between directors of these institutes, and the individual Provincials and Regents of Studies in order to advance their mission. This requires generosity in the perspective of the international mission of the Order. In addition, the institutions concerned must make themselves attractive to new professors and researchers. We petition the Master of the Order to assist the directors in seeking new professors and researchers for the renewal of these institutions.

École Biblique et Archéologique Française, Jérusalem

100. *[Exhortation]* In order to renew the mission of the École Biblique et Archéologique Française and in response of the request of the Chapter of Rome (cf. ACG 2010 Rome 110) the Master of the Order has developed a strategic plan in collaboration with the École Biblique. We exhort the École

Biblique to continue the implementation of this strategic plan, adopted in 2012. We further exhort the École Biblique to proceed with the development of the project "La Bible en Ses Traditions" (BEST).

Fribourg

101. *[Ordination]* Our mission in Fribourg is a project of collaboration by institutions under the immediate jurisdiction of the Master of the Order (couvent Saint Albert-le-Grand "Albertinum" and the Faculty of Theology) and the Province of Switzerland (couvent Saint-Hyacinthe and the studentate). Fribourg is an important place for the Order for both initial formation and post-graduate academic studies in Philosophy and Theology in the Dominican tradition. In order to strengthen the mission of the Order in Fribourg and in response to the request of the chapter of the Swiss Province (2010) for closer collaboration between the two convents of the Order in Fribourg, we ordain the Master of the Order and the Provincial of the Swiss Province to establish a commission with a view to the unification of the couvent Saint-Hyacinthe and the couvent Saint Albert-le-Grand.

The Historical Institute

102. *[Commission]* In the context of the Jubilee of 2016, we commission the Master of the Order to renew the Historical Institute. This renewal will take into account various aspects of the present situation, including the housing of the Historical Institute and its library in the facilities of the *PUST*, the archives of the Order at Santa Sabina, and the ongoing publications of the Institute. The Jubilee will also be an occasion to consider increased participation in, and prepa-ration of, colloquia and conferences. It can be envisaged that facilities will be available for students and scholars to visit the Institute to do research. This renewal is to be completed by the opening of the General Chapter in 2016, and a report submitted to that chapter.

The Pontifical University of St Thomas ("Angelicum")

103. *[Ordination]* As the viability of the Pontifical University of St Thomas Aquinas (PUST) in Rome becomes increasingly less certain, there is a serious concern about the University's future. There is an urgent need of restructuring. We ordain that the Rector continue and accelerate the restructuring that is necessary for the sustainability and renewed flourishing of the University with the support of the Master of the Order. This restructuring must include clarity about the mission of the University, its financial planning, fundraising, renewal of the faculties, their programs, their teaching staff and the recruitment of students. A process has already begun, including the revision of the statutes guided by the Master of the Order in response to the Chapter of Rome (ACG 2010 Rome: 120; cf. ACG 2010 Rome 118). The Rector should complete this restructuring by June 2015.

104. *[Commission]* We commission the Master of the Order, as Grand Chancellor, to implement the revised statutes immediately after their approval by the Holy See.

105. *[Petition]* We ask that the Master of the Order and the Rector of the PUST keep in mind the centers of studies of the Order affiliated or aggregated to the faculties of the PUST.

Other Entities

University of Santo Tomas

106. *[Congratulation]* Upon the 400th anniversary of the Pontifical University of Santo Tomas in Manila, we congratulate the brothers of the Province of Our Lady of the Most Holy Rosary and the Province of the Philippines for having nurtured and developed the University into a comprehensive university that is unique in the Order and that continues to play a major role in the growth of the Church and the Order in Asia.

Societas Editorum Dominicanorum

107. *[Congratulation]* We acknowledge with joy and further encourage the work of all the Dominican publishing houses that are members of the *Societas Editorum Dominicanorum*, following their fifth assembly hosted by the Éditions du Cerf in Paris, May 2013.

2016 Jubilee

108. *[Exhortation]* The Jubilee that we will celebrate in 2016 is a grace that the Lord grants us to renew the apostolic life of the Order, rooted in a profound and gentle listening to the Word of God and a caring attentiveness to the hopes of men and women today. For this reason we exhort all communities to take advantage of this occasion by reviewing their pastoral plans and renewing them with imagination, creativity, and freedom, paying particular attention to the following criteria:

> 1. To bring the Gospel to those excluded by society and to those estranged from the faith.

> 2. To share with one another the challenges of the mission and to work together.

> 3. To share the charism of preaching with others, especially the youth.

Mission Forums

109. *[Commission]* We commission the Socius of the Master of the Order for Apostolic Life to continue the "Mission Forums," which were initiated after the General Chapter of Rome, in response to a petition from the Master of the Order to the Provinces (cf Letter...). The purpose of these forums is to bring friars from around the world who are working in similar types of mission to share experiences and connect them with the best possible methodologies for their ministries.

110. *[Petition]* We petition Regional Socii and Prior Provincials to encourage the participation of the brothers in these forums and mission networks, not as one more job to do but as an incentive and a resource for the development of their own ministries.

111. *[Exhortation]* In view of the reports received by this Chapter and the questionnaires requested of the Provinces by the Master, we would like to underline a few particular challenges to the following mission contexts. We exhort brothers engaged in any of these areas of mission to keep these challenges in mind as they look ahead and plan for the future:

1. *Migrants:* to accompany migrants in the defense of their dignity and rights, and to analyze clearly and justly the varied causes of this phenomenon.

2. *Indigenous Peoples:* to accompany indigenous peoples and proclaim the Gospel to them; defend their dignity and identity; and to struggle against the exploitation of their living environment.

3. *Interreligious Dialogue:* to contribute to mutual understanding among the faithful of different religions; a task that has become urgent everywhere because of growing globalization and threats to peace.

4. *Ministry in City Centers:* to offer places of listening and meeting for those who are lonely and abandoned, as well as those who don't normally come to our churches.

5. *Pilgrimages and Devotion to the Rosary:* To make use of these traditional forms of Marian devotion in order to foster a vital relationship with Christ through meditation on the Gospel in the company of Mary.

6. *Parish Ministry:* to tend to the quality of our preaching and faith formation, as well as to seek out the youth and those who have become alienated from the faith.

7. *Education and Evangelization:* to find the best ways of communicating the faith and human values to young people who seek truth, freedom, and solidarity, with special attention to the protection of life, marriage, and the family.

Salamanca Process

112. *[Commission]* Among the projects developed after 2010, the "Salamanca Process" is of particular importance. It is a sustained process of collaboration between friars engaged in pastoral ministry and friars dedicated to academic study, as occurred in the 16th century between the missionaries in the New World and the friars of the Convent of St. Stephen in Salamanca. We commission the Socii to the Master of the Order for the Intellectual Life and the Apostolic Life to report to the Order the first steps taken in this direction and to foster its implementation in the diverse regions of the Order.

113. *[Petition]* We petition the Regents of Study to bring for discussion to their Provincial Councils in 2014 concrete proposals for the implementation of the "Salamanca Process," focusing on those topics that would be of particular interest to their Province. As a result of this discussion, each Province could take on one or more topics, organizing groups that bring together brothers engaged in pastoral ministry and those engaged in academic work, to find pertinent solutions that are faithful to the Gospel and can contribute to the renewal of the mission of their Province.

114. *[Exhortation]* We exhort the brothers to pay particular attention to certain areas of socio-cultural reality that render this dialogue especially urgent:

> 1. Areas of vulnerability: peoples and individuals whose life, dignity, and cultures are threatened (migrants, natives peoples, minorities, populations displaced by violence and the exploitation of resources, etc.).

> 2. Areas of the search for meaning and belonging: to seek to understand their causes, attendant difficulties and possible conflicts (for example, those arising from national, cultural, or religious identity, etc.)

> 3. The area of secularity: the abandonment of faith and religion; the area of agnosticism and indifference.

Internet

115. *[Ordination]* Bearing in mind that the internet is both a communications medium requiring technical expertise and a new area of communication requiring new methods and styles, we ordain the Provinces to name a promoter of media of communications, charged with the task of promoting and coordinating initiatives in this field at the level of each Province. Each promoter will inform the curia of his appointment in order to be included in the wider network "Order of Preachers for Technology, Information, and Communication" (OPTIC), under the coordination of the General Promoter for Communication.

116. *[Commission]* We commission the General Promoter for Communication to propose new means for working in the internet to brothers involved in the Salamanca Process and in the other Mission Forums.

Youth and the Dominican Youth Movement (DYM)

117. *[Petition]* The Dominican Youth Movement recently celebrated an international meeting in Bogota, Colombia. It currently exists in approximately 20 countries, yet it is still unknown in many entities. We petition Priors Provincial to promote the organization of DYM groups in their entities and to designate friars to accompany existing groups.

118. *[Exhortation]* We exhort all the brothers who work in youth ministry, especially with the DYM, to not only preach to the youth, but to also form them as preachers to their peers.

Other Topics

Journées Romaines Dominicaines

119. *[Congratulation]* We commend the relocation in 2014 of the *Journées Romaines Dominicaines* to Indonesia and we support the meeting of regional promoters of justice and peace in the Asia-Pacific Region on the same topic of Interreligious Dialogue.

Priestly Fraternities

120. *[Petition]* We petition priors provincial to accompany the members of Dominican priestly fraternities, and if it be the case to name a friar to help form these communities. We likewise petition that consideration be given to the possibility of including permanent deacons, whether in priestly fraternities or in lay fraternities.

The Meaning of Regional and Provincial Vicariates for the Mission of the Order

121. *[Commission]* We commission the Socii of the Master of the Order for different regions to prepare, together with their respective Provincials and Vicars, a report on the role that Regional and Provincial Vicariates have had in the Mission of the Order. This report should include vicariates that existed at the time of the General Chapter of Walberberg (1980). This report must be presented at the next General Chapter.

Foundation in Madagascar

122. *[Exhortation]* Twenty years ago, the Province of Toulouse founded a house in La Réunion. The Province is working toward strengthening its presence on this island in order to broaden its mission in the Indian Ocean region. We exhort the Prior Provincial with his council to favorably regard the apostolic needs of Madagascar, and to be in communication with the IAOP.

word.op.org

123. *[Congratulation and Commission]* We congratulate Friar Scott Steinkirchner for the valuable work that he has done on the www.word.op.org webpage and we commission the Promoter for Communications to extend and complete the translation of the webpage into Spanish and French.

CHAPTER VII: FORMATION

Ongoing Formation

124. *[Ordination]* Ongoing formation is increasingly necessary to understand and interpret the concerns of the world and the social and political reality of our time; to maintain hope and share faith; to grow in human and emotional integration; and to build a preaching community at the service of the People of God. Therefore we ordain the provincial promoters of permanent formation (LCO 251-ter) and conventual priors, assisted by the conventual lector, to organize, at least twice a year, ongoing formation meetings on these or similar issues proposed by members of the community, and which should benefit from the participation of the entire community.

125. *[Declaration]* We declare that permanent formation in the Order refers not only to the acquisition of knowledge following the end of formal institutional education, but also to the continuous process of maturation of the friar (cf. LCO 251-bis) and the edification of the Dominican community in all aspects of its existence.

126. *[Commission]* We commission the Priors Provincial and those responsible for permanent formation, in view of the jubilee, to encourage the communities of their entities to reflect on the theme "The Community in Relation to the Mission"; and to organize a provincial meeting on this topic between 2014 and 2015, in order to identify criteria to integrate these two fundamental dimensions of our life.

The Formation of Formators

127. *[Commission]* Given the importance of formation of the brothers in our current rapidly changing times, and taking into account the concerns about formation expressed by the Master of the Order in his *Relatio,* we commission the Master of the Order to delegate, as he sees fit, one of his current socii to handle affairs related with the formation of the friars.

128. *[Petition]* We petition the Master of the Order that the responsibilities of the socius delegated to the formation of the friars include the following:

> 1. To assist the master in promoting the initial and ongoing formation of clerical and cooperator brothers;

> 2. To assist in promoting community life in the Provinces;

> 3. To coordinate the redaction or modification of the *Ratio Formationis Generalis* as needed;

> 4. To promote the formation of formators.

129. *[Petition]* We petition the Master of the Order to entrust the socius delegated to the formation of the friars to elaborate, with the aid of a commission of experts named by the Master of the Order, a Curriculum for formators in order to prepare them for their work. It should be submitted for approval in 2014.

130. *[Petition]* We petition the Master of the Order to entrust the socius delegated to the formation of the friars with the design and organization, in 2014, of one or more workshops for recently named formators, where participants will reflect on the essential elements of formation, according to our Dominican tradition and charism, in order to help them do their work properly. (Cf. ACG 2004 Kraków 274, ACG 2010 Rome 191).

131. *[Congratulation and Commission]* We congratulate the regions that regularly organize meetings and courses for formators and we commission the IEOP to establish activities of this kind by 2016. (cf. ACG 2004 Kraków 272, ACG 2007 Bogotá 219, ACG 2010 Rome 192)

132. *[Petition]* We petition the Master of the Order, with the aid of the socius delegated to the formation of the friars, to present a new *Ratio Formationis Generalis* by 2016.

133. *[Commission]* We commission Provincial Chapters and Priors Provincial with their Councils that, when naming new formators, they do everything possible to ensure that the new formators begin their ministry at least six months after they are appointed, so that they can prepare to undertake this delicate and important service to the Order.

Dominican Maturity Training

134. *[Exhortation]* We are not born Dominicans; rather, we grow and gradually become Dominicans. Human, intellectual, spiritual, and emotional formation must occupy a special place so that we can carry out the preaching mission of the Order. Bearing this in mind, we exhort conventual priors and formators to reread and reflect on the texts regarding formation in LCO 164-176 and the Acts of the 2010 General Chapter of Rome 185-190, 195-197, and to implement them.

135. *[Exhortation]* Dominican maturity is expressed in the joyful living of the evangelical counsels and the virtues, to which we commit our lives through our religious profession (cf. Letter of Timothy Radcliffe, *Vowed to Mission*, 1994). We exhort our communities to pay special attention to reflection on and fidelity to our Dominican consecrated life, entering deeply into its contemplative dimension, the source of all our life and mission.

136. *[Exhortation]* Human and Dominican maturity require an atmosphere of respectful relationships, relational skills, mutual forgiveness, and confidence in the brother. We exhort superiors to carefully promote these conditions in formation communities.

137. *[Exhortation]* In Sacred Scripture, people's history is not forgotten but integrated into the history of salvation. Likewise, when a young man knocks at the door of our houses, we should also consider his history and ours. We should not be afraid to look at our past and that of young people. We should ask of them and of ourselves an attitude of openness and communication. We exhort superiors and members of formation communities to welcome one another with open hearts and minds.

138. *[Exhortation]* We exhort formators and members of formation communities not to favor ways and attitudes that impede the maturation of the young men we are forming. We must all learn to find support and mature answers to our problems within our communities, with an authentic and deep love for the Lord.

139. *[Commission]* Formation is a means to better serve humanity. For this reason, the desire to serve through preaching and availability for mission must be present from the start of Dominican life. We commission superiors, formators, and vocational promoters to take these criteria into account when engaging in vocational discernment, in order to prevent any sign of narcissism in the brothers in formation.

140. *[Commission]* We commission the priors and superiors of convents and houses of formation, that in agreement with formators, they encourage throughout the year – where this is still not done – informal meetings of professed brothers with those in formation, so that members of these communities might share and to get to know one another.

141. *[Commission]* Given the large number of elderly friars and of communities of increasingly higher median age, we commission the socius delegated to the formation of the friars to establish in the *Ratio Formationis Generalis* a section devoted to specific formation in how to fruitfully live this stage of life from a human and Dominican point of view, and to be able to preach from it and to it.

142. *[Commission]* We commission the socius delegated to the formation of the friars, when redrafting the *Ratio Formationis Generalis*, to bear in mind n. 349 of the General Chapter of Providence: "We ordain that in our program of initial formation there be serious reflection and sharing on affective life and maturity, sexuality, celibacy and chaste love." (ACG 2001 Providence 349).

Diversity and Cooperation in Formation

143. *[Exhortation]* We note and appreciate the diversity of environments in which our formation is done, as well as the need it has to respond to the unique conditions of each of our candidates and brothers in formation. We exhort those in charge of initial formation to take into account the criteria and challenges outlined in the Acts of the General Chapter of Bogotá as a guide to understand and work with that diversity (cf. ACG 2007 Bogotá 206-207).

144. *[Exhortation]* The time in preparation to enter the novitiate is employed by our entitites in different ways, depending on the conditions proper to each region. We exhort priors provincial to see that the Formation Council of their respective entities and their *Ratio Formationis Particularis* clarify the nature of the preparation time preceding entry into the novitiate, so that the novitiate retains its unique character of initiation into our Dominican religious life.

145. *[Commission]* The Order of Preachers was founded from the beginning to be useful for the salvation of all people, regardless of nationality, race, and language. We commission those responsible for formation in each entity to pay special attention to encouraging missionary vocations among all our student brothers and to promote interprovincial and international exchanges and ministerial and formation experiences during the time of initial formation, as noted by the General Chapter of Kraków (ACG 2004 Kraków 270).

146. *[Commission]* Dominican formation has a number of important requirements, namely: a strong community that is able to welcome; a conventual structure that is able to form; well trained formators; a cloister of active professors; and a sufficient number of brothers in formation. We commission Priors Provincial who lack these conditions in their Provinces to seek the means and ways to collaborate with other entities of the Order or to ensure that their brothers in formation are received by Provinces that meet these conditions.

Promotion of Dominican Vocations

147. *[Ordination]* Each vocation to Dominican life is a call from the Lord to the candidate, and a gift of the Lord to us. It is therefore necessary to promote and to take care of the vocations that God puts in our hands. We ordain that the Provinces that do not yet have a Provincial Promoter of Vocations, select a brother, preferably full-time, to fulfill this essential task (cf. ACG 2010 Rome 189).

148. *[Petition]* We petition Provincial Promoters of Vocations that they also promote vocations for the whole Dominican family in their work and that they collaborate with the Dominican family in this mission.

149. *[Exhortation]* To contemplate and to give to others that which has been contemplated is the greatest task of every Dominican. We exhort Priors Provincial and Provincial Promoters of Vocations that, during the selection process of our candidates, they make sure that the candidates show evidence of the following double desire: to listen to God and to serve the brethren through preaching. Special care should be taken of this in the case of candidates who come from other religious institutes or movements, from the secular clergy, or in the case of so-called "late vocations."

150. *[Declaration]* We declare that the emergence of a renewed way of living the cooperator brother vocation is occurring in the Order (cf. *Study on Cooperator Brothers*, [in progress]). They are Dominican religious who assume the preaching of the common priesthood of the faithful (cf. LCO 1 § VI). This new experience challenges us particularly to recognize cooperator brothers as preachers in the full sense.

151. *[Exhortation]* We exhort the friars, and especially promoters of vocations and formators to value, embrace, and promote the vocation of the cooperator brother in our Order (cf. ACG 2007 Bogotá 212).

152. *[Petition]* On the occasion of the Jubilee, we petition the Master of the Order to promote the writing of the history of cooperator brothers in the Order, so that this vocation and the various ways of living it out may be better known and appreciated.

153. *[Petition]* We petition Priors Provincial and those responsible for formation in all the entities of the Order that they take into account in forming cooperator brothers the rich legislation on this subject in the LCO and the Acts of the General Chapters (cf. LCO 217-220; ACG 1998 Bologna 139; ACG 2004 Kraków 250-254,258; ACG 2007 Bogotá 212-213; ACG 2010 Rome 198).

Restructuring of the Order

154. *[Ordination]* The process of restructuring begun by the General Chapter of Rome (2010) is intended to strengthen the mission of the Order as part of its renewal in the light of the coming Jubilee. In view of the fact that the Order is composed of Provinces (LCO 252), we ordain that the Master of the Order and all brothers of the entities concerned continue this process of reorganization of the structure of government (ACG 2010 Rome 201), in order to promote the apostolic mission and regular observance of the brethren. At the end of this process, which should be completed in 2016, there will be, as autonomous entities of the Order, only Provinces and Vice Provinces. Convents and houses under the immediate jurisdiction of the Master of the Order will also exist. At the provincial level, in addition to convents and houses in the territory of the Province, some Provinces will have Provincial Vicariates, as well as convents and houses outside of the territory of the Province. Moreover, all currently existing Regional Vicariates are to be designated Provincial Vicariates at the end of this process. Those convents or houses which are not integrated into a Province or a Provincial Vicariate at the end of this process are to be recognized as communities outside the territory of the Province. The Prior Provincial is to make an annual visitation to these communities and may name for such convents and houses a Vicar (cf. LCO 345).

155. *[Ordination]* We ordain that the Master and his council no longer establish any General Vicariate.

156. *[Ordination]* In order to strengthen Dominican life and mission, we ordain that by 2016 all General Vicariates conform to one of the entities of the Order outlined in Ordination n. 1. Each General Vicariate, with the assistance of the General Council, is to continue the process outlined in Act 206 of the General Chapter of Rome 2010.

157. *[Exhortation]* Having in mind that "there is now no longer Jew nor Greek... for you are all one in Christ Jesus" (Gal 3:28), we exhort brothers of the entities that are or could be involved in a collaborative process to provide or to accept timely assistance in a spirit of fraternity to or from entities in the same region, and not to allow national feelings or historical memories to militate against the establishment and strengthening of the mission of the Order, which is the preaching of charity.

158. *[Petition]* We petition the Master of the Order to present to the next General Chapter a proposal for the government of those remaining General Vicariates that have not been able to complete this process.

159. *[Ordination]* We ordain that each Province or Vice Province not currently fulfilling the conditions in LCO 253 § I or LCO 257 § I, 1° continue to determine what juridical structure would best energize its Dominican way of life and mission.

160. *[Constitution]* The Chapter believes that for Provinces and Vice Provinces which are declining in numbers, the burdens of government can weigh too heavily and some special provision may need to be made. Reducing Provinces to Vice Provinces is not always sufficient, and it will no longer be possible after 2016 to reduce either to a General Vicariate, which in any case does not liberate the brothers for the mission of the Order.

We therefore inchoate with an ordination the following:

LCO 258 § I.–If for a period of three years, a Province or Vice Province does not fulfill the conditions established by LCO 253 § I or by LCO 257 § I, the General Chapter or the Master of the Order with the consent of his council may declare that it no longer enjoys the rights and obligations of a Province or Vice Province, always with the exception of the right to participate in a General Chapter that has already been convoked.

§ II.–This declaration having been made, if a Province fulfill the conditions of LCO 257 § I, it enjoys the rights and obligations of a Vice Province. Otherwise, the Master of the Order, having heard the brothers, shall institute as superior of this Province or Vice Province, for four years, a Vicar, being a brother who must fulfill the conditions required to be a provincial and who will govern it according to norms established by the Master of the Order.

§ III.–When a Province or Vice Province which had lost the rights of a Province or Vice Province as provided for in § I, shall once again, for a period of three years, have the necessary conditions, the General Chapter or the Master of the Order shall declare that it enjoys all its rights as a Province or Vice Province.

§ IV.–In regions where, because of adverse circumstances, a Provincial Chapter cannot be held, the Master of the Order, with the consent of his council, may provide for its equitable representation at the General Chapter.

161. *[Petition]* We petition the Master, when considering the establishment of new Vice Provinces (cf. LCO 257) to have particular concern for the need of a Vice Province to have all the resources necessary for a proper autonomy in matters of government, formation, study and economy.

Government for Mission

162. *[Exhortation]* We exhort Provinces that have Provincial vicariates or other missions outside their territory to ensure in their apostolic planning that the strength of the mission is not weakened, and to ensure that the brothers in the missions have the necessary fraternal support, opportunities for common study and the other features proper to authentic Dominican life.

163. *[Exhortation]* The biblical experience of a jubilee was marked by a spirit of generosity, manifested for example in the remission of debts. In anticipation of the Order's 800th Jubilee, we exhort all Provinces of the Order, in the same spirit of generosity, to consider ways in which they can offer assistance to weaker entities: this assistance might take the form of providing some or all initial formation, financial support or

assignations of brothers, or even to the establishment of a convent in the territory of the weaker entity. Even weaker entities might consider giving out of their poverty.

164. *[Exhortation]* We exhort those Provinces that do not have a significant experience or culture of external mission to consider ways in which their missionary spirit may be developed.

165. *[Commendation]* We recommend that, where two entities of the Order are involved in a shared mission, with one entity providing assistance to another, the two enter into a carefully considered contract of collaboration.

166. *[Exhortation]* We exhort Provinces intending to establish missions outside their territory to take care to ensure that they do so on the basis of a carefully considered and realistic plan.

Provincial and Regional Vicariates

167. *[Ordination]* We ordain that every Province having a Provincial or Regional Vicariate, at its next Provincial Chapter, shall consider whether such Vicariates fulfill the conditions necessary according to our laws, and proceed to make such institutional changes as are required in regard to existence, nomenclature and statute.

168. *[Ordination]* In view of LCO 362 § IV and LCO 384 § II, 1° we ordain that the Master of the Order, when approving the Acts of a Provincial Chapter, shall ensure that the Statute of a Vicariate permits a necessary autonomy to the Vicariate in view of its distinct cultural and geographical circumstances, while also making the strongest possible provision for the proper concern for and support of the mission in the Vicariate by the Province.

169. *[Petition]* We petition the Master of the Order, during the next year, to establish a meeting between Provincials of Provinces with Provincial Vicariates and the Vicars Provincial, to seek ways of strengthening the structural links between Provinces and Vicariates and of ensuring that the brothers in the

Vicariates receive the necessary supports for living fully authentic Dominican lives.

170. *[Constitution]* Wishing to affirm that Provincial Vicariates are entities of Provinces and should be bound more closely in their government to the Provinces to which they belong; wishing to avoid a certain separation that may emerge as a result of their separate representation at General Chapters; and wishing to avoid double representation of brothers at General Chapters, we inchoate the following:

> 1. LCO 407 § I, 5° and LCO 407 § I, 6°: Delete the words "excluding, however, those who are assigned in vicariates";
>
> 2. Delete LCO 407 § I, 7°;
>
> 3. Delete LCO 408, 5°;
>
> 4. Delete LCO 409, 5°;
>
> 5. Delete LCO 409-bis.

171. *[Commendation]* A General Chapter benefits from the contributions of brothers involved in many and various missions. We therefore recommend that the Master of the Order ensure that the concerns of brethren ministering in new foundations, Provincial Vicariates and other fields of mission be heard at General Chapters either by way of an invitation to attend as guests or by some other suitable means such as gathering information from them by way of surveys in preparation for the Chapter.

172. *[Constitution]* Wishing to affirm that General Chapters are meetings of the entities of the Order, which is to say, Provinces and Vice Provinces (cf. LCO 252; 405), and that all brothers should be represented by these Provinces or Vice Provinces at General Chapters, and wishing to avoid double representation of brothers at General Chapters, we inchoate the following:

1. LCO 407 § I, 5° and LCO 407 § I, 6°: Delete the words "and those directly assigned to houses under the immediate jurisdiction of the Master of the Order";

2. Delete LCO 407 § I, 8°;

3. Delete LCO 407-bis;

4. Delete LCO 408, 6°;

5. Delete LCO 409, 6°;

6. Delete LCO 409-ter;

7. LCO 497 § I, 2° Delete the words "unless the provincial statutes stipulate otherwise".

173. *[Constitution]* We abrogate the insertion into LCO 257 § I, 1° made by the General Chapter of Rome 2010.

Particular Entities

174. *[Exhortation]* We warmly appreciate the continued development of the "2016 project" in which the entities of the *Junta Iberica de Provincias [JIP]* are engaged, and we exhort all the brothers involved to continue the process, implementing opportunely the decisions they have reached, and having particular concern for the care and development of their Provincial Vicariates. Recognizing that the process may imply the unification of some entities, we exhort all the members of the *JIP* to participate in a common planning of the mission of the Order in that region.

175. *[Petition]* We renew the petition made by the General Chapter of Rome (AGC 2010 Rome 211) and we ask the Provincial Priors of the Provinces of Betica and of the Holy Rosary to continue and strengthen the collaboration between both Vicariates in Venezuela in order to prepare the erection of a Vice Province.

176. *[Congratulation]* We congratulate the brothers involved in the establishment of the Vice Province of Bolivia.

177. *[Exhortation]* We exhort the brothers working in the region of the Caribbean to cooperate more closely with one another with a view to establishing fully authentic Dominican life and mission. We also exhort those Provinces that have missions in the Caribbean to establish a process of cooperation for the strengthening of Dominican life and mission in the region.

178. *[Recommendation]* We recommend a yearly meeting among the vicars in the region of the Caribbean, and priors of priories in the region outside the territory of their Provinces with the *Socius* for Latin America and the Caribbean to explore collaboration and apostolic ministry.

179. *[Exhortation]* We exhort the Provinces in Latin America to revitalise their missionary spirit in support of the existing Provincial Vicariates in the region by the sending of friars, economic help or other forms of collaboration in apostolic projects.

180. *[Congratulation]* We congratulate the Province of St John the Baptist in Peru and the Regional Vicariate of Santa Rosa (Province of Spain in Peru) for the collaboration between their centers of formation and pastoral activities, and we encourage them to make progress towards the goal of a single Dominican Province in Peru.

181. *[Congratulation]* We congratulate the Province of the Netherlands for having invited the Province of England to erect a house in the territory of the Netherlands.

182. *[Petition]* We petition the Province of England to make every effort to accept this invitation and to make it an important aspect of its apostolic planning.

General Chapters

183. *[Commission]* We commission the Master of the Order, with the General Council, to review the procedures for General Chapters. In particular, they are to consider:

> 1. Whether memberships of Commissions might be proposed three months in advance of the Chapter, with proposed presidents being given contact details for other members with a view to initiating initial discussions;

> 2. Whether clear guidelines might be produced, and distributed three months in advance, on the general procedure and function of the work of Chapter commissions, including their responsibilities with regard to petitions to the Chapter;

> 3. Whether more detailed suggestions might be proposed by the General Council to each Commission concerning the particular questions they might consider and what decisions might be required.

> 4. Whether more clearly directed preparation by vocals might make it possible to reduce the duration of a General Chapter.

184. *[Commission]* We commission the Master of the Order to commission a study regarding the General Chapter, keeping the following in mind:

> 1. Frequency of Chapters (e.g. an elective chapter every 12 years or every 10 years, or some other configuration);

> 2. Reduction of the number of commissions;

> 3. Preparatory instrument(s);

> 4. Improved means of communication (i.e. virtual, internet);

> 5. Costs;

6. Legislative/juridical aspects;

7. Reception of the Acts in the life of the Order.

This study should be disseminated one year before the next General Chapter.

Visitations

185. *[Petition]* We petition the Master of the Order to continue to seek the most fruitful means for visitations of Provinces according to ACG 2010 Rome: 222-224, and in particular that he allot sufficient time to visitate larger Provinces.

Electronic Voting

186. *[Ordination]* We ordain that the Master of the Order, by the end of 2014, prepare guidelines for the use of secure electronic voting as an alternative to postal voting in all cases where postal voting is permitted by our constitutions.

Lay Fraternities

187. *[Ordination]* We ordain that, when a Prior Provincial wishes to nominate as Provincial Promoter for the Lay Fraternities or as Religious Assistant for one or more Fraternity someone who is under a jurisdiction other than that of the brothers of the Order, this shall only take place with the prior written agreement of the competent authority. We also ask the Master of the Order to insert this condition into the norms of the Lay Fraternities.

188. *[Ordination]* We ordain that the directories of the Dominican Laity, national or Provincial, be approved by the Provincial with his Council in the Province(s) in which these entities are established.

Chapter IX: Financial Administration

189. *[Declaration]* We declare that the syndic of the Order, fr. Hilario Provecho Álvarez, OP, in accordance with LCO 569, presented a report of his administration from his appointment until now. The report was approved.

190. *[Declaration]* We declare that the syndic of the Order, fr. Hilario Provecho Álvarez, OP, in accordance with LCO 569, presented the accounts of the General Curia for the fiscal years 2010-2012. These accounts were approved.

191. *[Declaration]* We declare that the syndic of the Order, fr. Hilario Provecho Álvarez, OP, in accordance with LCO 572, presented the personal accounts of the Master of the Order. These accounts were approved.

192. *[Declaration]* We declare that the syndic of the Order, fr. Hilario Provecho Álvarez, OP, presented the following accounts:

1. Solidarity Fund.
2. Saint Dominic Fund.
3. Francisco de Vitoria Fund.
4. Dominique Renouard Fund.
5. Master of the Order Fund.
6. Leonine Commission Fund.
7. Administrative Funds for the entities under the immediate jurisdiction of the Master of the Order.

These accounts were approved.

193. *[Declaration]* We declare that, in accordance with LCO 571, the financial reports of the convents and institutions under the immediate jurisdiction of the Master of the Order, promptly sent to the Master, were approved by their respective councils. These reports have been thoroughly studied by the Economic Council of the Order and approved by the Master of the Order and the General Council.

194. *[Declaration]* We declare that the syndic of the Order with the economic council drafted the Administrative Statutes of the Order, which was submitted and approved by the general council of the Order (cf. ACG 2010 Rome 244 and LCO 553).

195. *[Declaration]* We declare that the solidarity office *Spem Miram Internationalis* was created, whose purpose is to manage requests for solidarity assistance, in accordance with the statutes approved by the Master and his Council (cf. AGC Rome 231).

196. *[Declaration]* We declare that the *International Dominican Foundation* (IDF) falls under the purview of the office of solidarity of the Order.

197. *[Declaration]* We declare that the Master of the Order and the general council have given the Angelicum the amount of one million Euros from the solidarity fund to cover building repairs (cf. AGC 2010 Rome 252).

Courses of Action

198. *[Ordination]* We ordain the Master of the Order to include the following in the *Ratio Studiorum Generalis* (RSG): Initial formation of student brothers should include training in financial and administrative matters.

199. *[Ordination]* We ordain that the socii of the Master of the Order organize regional meetings of the syndics of the entities in their region around every three years. These meetings will assist in training and the exchange of ideas regarding economic policies.

200. We confirm ordination n. 248 of the Acts of Rome, which appears in italics in the following text:

"*[Ordination]* We ordain that the following replace LCO 567: Priors Provincial, Vice Provincials, Vicars General and heads of institutions under the immediate jurisdiction of the

Master of the Order, assisted by their Syndics, are responsible for sending directly to the Master of the Order by 31 August each year the following two documents:

1° The Annual Economic Report. This is a comprehensive presentation of the economic situation of the entity. It shall include details of income, expenses, assets, liabilities, and annual budgets as well as major projects undertaken or planned. If the entity has different *vicariates, priories*, houses, or institutes, this report shall give details of the economic situation of each one. The format of this report may vary according to local custom but must include all of the information requested above. A sample format shall be available from the office of the Syndic of the Order.

2° The Contributions (tax-deduction) Questionnaire. This is used to calculate the annual contributions from the entities of the Order. On the basis of this questionnaire entities claim their allowable deductions for formation expenses, donations to other entities of the Order *and medical and health care expenses of the brethren*. The questionnaire shall be sent out each year by the Syndic of the Order and its format shall be the same for every entity."

Order Contributions

201. We confirm ordination no. 249 of the Acts of Rome:

> *[Ordination] We ordain that the annual contribution of each Province, Vice Province and General Vicariate be assessed according to the formula approved in the Acts of the General Chapter of Bogotá 2007, n. 261. To this formula will be included the medical and health care costs with the same criteria as for the costs of formation.*

202. *[Ordination]* We ordain that the amount of expenditures that the Master of the Order may authorize without needing the approval of his council, shall not exceed € 75,000.

203. *[Ordination]* We ordain that the president of the solidarity office of the Order, *Spem Miram Internationalis*, submit an annual report on the solidarity funds to Priors Provincial, Vice Provincials, and Vicars General.

204. *[Commission]* We commission the Master of the Order that, within the framework of the General Council of November 2013, he coordinate a joint meeting between the President of IDF and the General Council, in order to analyze the current status of IDF, the subsidies it will give to projects of the Order, and the possibility of IDF not receiving an annual subsidy.

205. *[Ordination]* We ordain that the syndic of the Order include in the budget of the General Curia an annual subsidy to the following entities:

1. University of St. Thomas (Angelicum): € 150,000 intended for ordinary operating expenses.

2. To the Convent of St. Dominic and St. Sixtus at the Angelicum: € 40,000 (ACG 2007 Bogotá 276), which will cover the expenses of friars assigned *simpliciter*.

3. Inter-Africa (IAOP): € 150,000 proportionally distributed according to the number of friars in each sub-region, for the initial formation of the friars.

4. Asia/Pacific: € 50,000 for formation projects and regional projects.

5. Latin America and the Caribbean (CIDALC): € 25,000 for regional projects.

6. Central and Eastern Europe: € 25,000 for regional projects.

7. International Dominican Foundation (IDF): a maximum of € 75,000 annually (until the outcome of the study of the joint meeting in November).

206. *[Ordination]* We ordain that the ordinary contribution of every Province, Vice Province, and general vicariate to the General Curia be no less than € 3000.

207. *[Ordination]* We ordain that the contribution of convents and other institutions under the immediate jurisdiction of the Master of the Order be 6% of their gross revenues.

Costs of the Chapter

208. *[Ordination]* We ordain that the cost of the General Chapter should be shared equitably, reflecting the portion that each entity contributes annually to the regular budget of the Order. Transportation costs are divided equally among all, and administrative costs proportionally. Each delegate must pay the actual *per diem* cost (ACG 2007 Bogotá 286; ACG 2010 Rome 260).

209. *[Exhortation]* We exhort Provinces, convents, and houses to utilize their assets in a spirit of solidarity and according to the criterion of service to all the friars and all persons in need.

Appreciation

210. *[Thanksgiving]* We thank the syndic of the Order, fr. Hilario Provecho Álvarez, OP, and the Economic Council for his enormous contribution to the betterment of the economic administration of the Order by introducing the digital signature, the submission of reports through the virtual cloud, and the simplification of the questionnaire for the contributions' chart.

211. NOTES

To present a clearer picture of changes in LCO made by the Chapter, the same procedure is used as was employed in the Acts of previous General chapters.[1]

The numerical order of the LCO is followed. At each number specific signs show whether the text was approved for the first second or third time.

***	a confirmed constitution (three chapters)
**	an approved constitution (two chapters)
*	an introduced constitution (one chapter)

(Note: If the approval or introduction of a constitution was made with an ordination, it is indicated by the sign [O] .

✦✦ Ordination voted on for the second time, abrogating a previous ordination

✦ Ordination accepted for the first time

[A] A text that is abrogated

New texts are printed in *italics*.

Since a good interpretation of changes made demands a knowledge of the preceding text and its history, reference to the preceding chapter is made with the following signs:

C = Caleruega, 1995
B = Bologna, 1998
P = Providence, 2001
K = Kraków, 2004
Bo = Bogotá, 2007
R = Roma, 2010

---

[1] Cf. ACG of Rome [1986], n. 307; Dublin, n. 188; Oakland, n. 208; Mexico, n. 248; Caleruega, ch. IX, p. 90; Bologna, n. 240; Providence, ch. X, p. 149; Kraków, n. 352, Bogotá, n. 288, and finally Rome [2010], n. 262.

This chapter sometimes changes texts "technically" although the substance of the law is not changed. The abbreviation "Techn." will mark such changes made whether to accommodate our laws to the CIC, or to harmonize the texts with other numbers of the LCO, or for a simple change in the rendering.

In our legislation what is said about convents applies also to houses unless expressly stipulated otherwise (LCO 260 § II).

In our legislation according to the purpose of LCO 252-256, by the name "Province" is included proportionally Vice Provinces and General Vicariates (LCO appendix n. 11).

212. (Bo 292; R 265)

*** 93. Const.–§ III.–The regent is proposed by the Provincial Chapter and is appointed by the Master of the Order for a ~~four-year term~~ *until the beginning of the following chapter. He can be proposed immediately for a second term, not however for a third.* While he is in office...

213. (Techn.)

96. Ord.–The Masterate in Sacred Theology is conferred on those brethren who are recognized as eminent in promoting ~~sciences, especially~~ the Sacred Sciences.

214. (Techn.)

97. Ord.–§ I. For anyone to be promoted to the Masterate in Sacred Theology, it is required:
3° that he be presented by the commission on the intellectual life to the Provincial Chapter *of the Province of affiliation or of assignation of the brother* and that he be proposed by two-thirds of the vocals of the same chapter, or ~~by the chapter of the Province of affiliation according to the same manner of proceeing or~~ by the Master of the Order, if this concerns a brother living in a convent or institute immediately subject to him; (K 356)

215. (Techn.)

138. Ord.–The brethren approved in the Order's examination for hearing confessions, by the very fact of their approval given in writing by the examiners, have delegated jurisdiction over persons subject to the Order, except nuns, and over others living day and night in our ~~houses~~ *convents* (Can. 967-969)

216. (R 266)

✦✦ 139. Ord.–The brethren shall keep ever in mind the fact that their public statements (in books, newspapers, radio, and television, *and other forms of mass media*) reflect not only on themselves but on their brothers, the Order, and the Church. For this reason, they should be particularly attentive to developing a sense of dialogue and mutual responsibility with their brothers and with their superiors in arriving at an opinion. They should pay special attention to this critical dialogue with major superiors if their statements or writings deal with disputed matters of some importance.

217. (Techn.)

LCO 159. Ord.–The Master has responsibility for both the spiritual life and for discipline in so far as both are required for the full instruction of those to be formed, leaving to them, moreover, the freedom of approaching other ~~priests~~ *brothers* for more personal spiritual direction.

218. (Techn.)

180. Const.– § II.–The Master of the Order, with the consent of his council, can concede in particular cases and by way of exception that a candidate can make the novitiate in another ~~house~~ *convent* of the Order under the guidance of an approved religious who assumes the role of master of novices (cf. CIC 647 § 2).

III.–The major superior can permit a group of novices to live for a stated period of time which he designates in another ~~house~~ *convent* of the Order (cf. CIC 647 § 3).

219. (Techn.)

LCO 247. Ord.–§ II.–They should not fail to question each of those to be ordained *and to receive from them a declaration written in his own hand and signed, cf. CIC 1036,* to make more certain that they freely and knowingly want to be promoted to orders in the religious state.~~(cf. CIC 1036)~~.

220.

◆   256-bis. Ord.–§ I– For the union *or fusion* of ~~two~~ *several* entities ~~(Provinces, Vice Province or vicariates)~~ the following

1° ~~The vote of the council of each entity~~ *a consultative vote* in regard to ~~mutual~~ matters concerning the union *or fusion*
2° *To the extent that the joinings require.* consultations of the brethren ~~and the chapters of all the convents and houses in the same entities~~, *of the entities which are involved* in a manner worked out or approved *by the Master General* ~~in the individual entities~~.
3° ~~A special statute approved by the Master of the Order for the celebration of a chapter of each entity, in which the entities vote whether the union is to be proposed to the Master of the Order and for the celebration of the first meeting of the new entity after the manner of a chapter.~~
4° ~~The decision of the Master of the order with his council; the first superior of the new entity is appointed by the master of the order.~~
§ II–~~The union of two entities and the union or fusion of several entities should be done in the way described in I, with appropriate changes being made.~~ *If it seems necessary, a special statute of provisions can be promulgated by the Master of the Order.*
§ III.–In the case of the division of a Province, the manner of proceeding shall be worked out by the provincial council

and approved by the Master of the Order with his council. ~~(B, n. 254)~~

221. (R 268)

** [A]   257. Const.-§ II. ~~In a territory where no Province or Vice Province exists, because of local needs or the firm hope of implanting the Order in a permanent manner, the Master of the Order, having consulted first the brothers assigned to the vicariate and having consulted the council of the pertinent Province, can, with the consent of his council, establish a general vicariate with a determined territory, which shall be governed by statutes prepared by the vicariate and approved by the Master of the Order and his council. In this case, having consulted the brothers of the vicariate, a vicar general is appointed the first time by the Master of the Order for four years. Relations between this general vicariate and other vicariates which may exist in the same place shall be determined according to n. 395.~~

222. (R 269)

* [A]   Const. 258.-§ I. ~~If any Province for a period of three years shall not have three convents or thirty-five vocals assigned in the Province and habitually living there, the Master of the Order, having consulted his council, shall declare that it no longer enjoys the right of participating in General Chapters as a Province and shall reduce it to a Vice Province or to a general vicariate (B-255) according to the norm of n.257, I, unless a General Chapter shall already have been convoked. § II. When a Province which has been reduced to a Vice Province as in § I for a period of three years shall again have the necessary conditions, the Master of the Order must declare that it enjoys all its rights.~~

* [O]   258 Const.-§ I.–*If any Province or Vice Province for a period of three years to the norm of n. 253 or n. 257 § I does not fulfill the conditions requisite, the General Chapter or Master of the Order consulting with his council may declare it hardly*

large enough to enjoy the rights of the Province or Vice Province, saving always the right to participate in a General Chapter already convoked.

§ II. This declaration having been published, if the Province fulfills the requisite conditions by the norm of n. 257 § I, it would enjoy the rights and is bound to the obligations of a Vice Province. Otherwise the Master of the Order in and over this Province or Vice Province msy institute a vicar (cf. n. 400) for four years, who would have all the requisite conditions for a Prior Provincial, and rules this entity according to the norms established by the Master of the Order.

§ III. If afterwards the Province or Vice Province about which in § I fulfills the requisite conditions by the norm of n. 257 § I, the General Chapter or Master of the Order with the consent of his council may declare it to enjoy the rights of a Vice Province and to be bound to its obligations.

§ III. § IV.–In regions...

223. (Techn.)

A brother who according to the norm of § I ~~vel § III,~~ has been assigned simply to a Province, needs besides *as soon as possible* an assignment to a definite convent.

224. (R 270)

❖ ❖   285 Ord.–§ I.–Ordinations which have remained in force through ~~five~~ *two* successive chapters and in the ~~sixth~~ *third* have been approved, shall be inserted in the book of constitutions and ordinations. *If they had not been inserted, they are considered to be abrogated, unless they are instituted again by the General Chapter.*

225. (Techn.)

297-bis. Ord.–In transacting business, that factor has the force of law which, the majority of those who must be convoked being present, is satisfactory to the majority absolutely, that is, which exceeds half the number of votes cast without counting invalid votes and abstentions. ~~canon 127, paragraph I, being observed.~~

226. (R 272)

◆◆   328 Ord.–§ I.–Any brother enjoying active voice can be appointed syndic of the convent provided he is truly qualified for this office.

§ II.–*He is appointed by the prior with the consent of his council and with the approval of the Prior Provincial.*

§ ~~II.~~ III He is appointed for a three-year period and can be appointed immediately for another three years but not for a third time except ~~with the consent of the Prior Provincial~~ *in case of necessity.*

227. (R 273)

** [A]   332. Const.–§ I. A superior of a house is appointed for three years by the Prior Provincial, having consulted the brethren of the house, ~~or by the regional prior if this concerns a brother assigned in a regional vicariate and unless the statutes of the vicariate provide otherwise.~~ He can be appointed in the same manner for another three years immediately following, but not for a third time.
II.   The three-year period having elapsed, the Prior Provincial ~~or regional prior~~ is obliged to appoint a superior within a month. However, a superior of a house shall remain in office until his successor is present in the house, unless the Prior Provincial shall have determined otherwise.

228. (R 275)

◆ ◆ [A]   373. Ord.–Among other things, the following must be dealt with in the provincial council:
1° the appointment or removal of a regional prior and of a conventual prior;

79

2° the presentation or removal of a pastor, ~~the chapter of the community to which the parish is entrusted having been consulted~~.
3°-7° (as in the text)

229. (Techn.)

352. Ord.–The vocals of a Provincial Chapter are:
§ I.–1° regional priors;
   [...]
6° a delgate of a non-prioral house with at least four brothers enjoying active voice in the territory of any nation where there is not *another convent or* another house of the same Province. (B, n. 263; P, n. 492)
   [...]

230. (Bo 303; R 276)

378. Const.–§ I.–In each Province there shall be a syndic who shall have charge of the goods of the Province in accord with the norms established for administration.

***   § II.–*The brother who has been performing this duty may be immediately appointed again, not however for a third time.*

** [O]   *unless with the consent of the Master of the Order.*

231. (Bo 303; R 276)

** [A]   384. Const.–~~§ I–When a Province has outside its own territory in some nation or region at least fifteen vocals and one convent properly so called, a Provincial Chapter can unite them into a regional vicariate so that the apostolic activity and regular life of the brethren can be better coordinated.~~
~~II. It pertains to a regional vicariate: 1° to have its own statutes approved by a Provincial Chapter; 2° to celebrate its own chapters accord ing to the norm of the vicariate statutes; 3° to admit candidates to the novitiate and to first profession. 4° to admit to solemn profession and sacred~~

~~orders unless there is another provision in the provincial statute.~~

232. (R 277)

* [O] 384. Const. § I.–*When a Province has outside of its territory in another nation or region at least two houses of which one is a convent properly called, and at least fifteen vocals, the Provincial Chapter can combine them into a provincial vicariate, so that the apostolic activities and regular life of the brethren there may the better be able to be coordinated*

** [O] *§ II.–The provincial vicariate is regulated by a statute drawn up by the Provincial Chapter and approved by the Master of the Order.*

233.

◆ *384-bis. Ord.–The statutes of the vicariate ought to determine the norms*
    1° on the celebration of the chapter of the vicariate;
    2° on the office of the Vicar provincial who presides over the vicariate as vicar of the Prior Provincial;
    3° on the officials of the Vicariate;
    4° on the formation and promotion of vocations;
    5° on the right to participate ex officio in the provincial council and Provincial Chapter (cf. 352 § I, 1°), with active voice or not;
    6° on the faculties which the Vicar of the Prior Provincial, having heard his council, is able to grant, on the admission of candidates to the novitiate and to simple profession, on the assignment of brothers to a house and convent of the vicariate, on the confirmation of conventual priors and the appointment of superiors of houses.

234. (Techn.)

385. Const.–§ II–1° A regional prior is elected for four years by the vocals assigned in ~~the vicariate~~ *the convents of the*

vicariate and is confirmed by the Prior Provincial with the consent of his council;

235. (R 278)

✦ ✦ [A] 389. Ord.-~~Where the conditions for a regional vicariate indicated in n.384 above are wanting, a Provincial Chapter can establish a provincial vicariate and draw up a special statute for it. otherwise, having consulted the brethren, a Vicar Provincial shall be appointed by the Prior Provincial.~~

236. (Techn.)

407. Const. –The following are assembled and have voice in an elective chapter:
§ I.–In the election of the Master of the Order:
1°–4° (as in the text)
5° a socius of the Diffinitor of a General Chapter from Provinces having at least one hundred professed religious, excluding, however, those ~~who are assigned in vicariates~~ *assigned to convents of the vicariates* and those directly assigned to ~~houses~~ *convents* under the immediate jurisdiction of the Master of the Order;
6° a socius of the Prior Provincial going to a General Chapter from Provinces having at least four hundred professed religious, excluding, however, those ~~who are assigned in vicariates~~ *assigned to convents of the vicariate*; and those directly assigned to ~~houses~~ *convents* under the immediate jurisdiction of the Master of the Order;
7° a delegate from a Province having at least twenty-five and up to one hundred brothers assigned in ~~vicariates~~ *convents of the vicariate [assigned]* or ~~houses~~ *convents* of the Province outside the boundaries of the Province, elected from among them and by them according to provincial statute; furthermore, from a Province having one hundred one to two hundred brothers assigned in ~~vicariates~~ *convents of the vicariates*, another shall be elected delegate and so on in succession.
8° from among brethren directly assigned to ~~houses~~ *convents* under the immediate jurisdiction of the Master of

the Order, two delegates if they total less than one hundred, three delegates if they total one hundred or more, chosen according to the norm of n. 407-bis.

237. (R 279)

407. Const.–407.   The following are assembled and have voice in an elective chapter:
§ I.–In the election of the Master of the Order:
1°–3° (as in the text)

** [A]   4° Vice Provincial priors ~~and vicars general~~, concerning which in n. 257;
5°–6° (as in the texts with technical changes)

** [O]   7° a delegate from a Province having at least twenty-*five* and up to one hundred brothers assigned in vicariates or houses of their Province outside the boundaries of the Province, elected from among them and by them according to provincial statute; furthermore, from a Province having one hundred one to two hundred brothers assigned in vicariates, another shall be elected delegate and so on in succession.
8° (as in the text)

238.

407. I. The following are assembled and have voice in an elective chapter:
      § I.–In the election of a Master of the Order:
      1°-4°   (as in the text with changes introduced in the previous number)

* [A]   5° a socius of the Diffinitor of a General Chapter from Provinces having at least one hundred professed religious~~; excluding, however, those who are assigned in vicariates and those directly assigned to houses under the immediate jurisdiction of the Master of the Order;~~

* [A]   6° a socius of the Prior Provincial going to a General Chapter from Provinces having at least four hundred professed religious, ~~excluding, however, those who are~~

83

assigned in vicariates; and those directly assigned to houses under the immediate jurisdiction of the Master of the Order;

* [A]   7°-a delegate from a Province having at least ten and up to one hundred brothers assigned in vicariates or houses of the Province outside the boundaries of the Province, elected from among them and by them according to provincial statute; furthermore, from a Province having one hundred and one to two hundred brothers assigned in vicariates, another shall be elected delegate and so on in succession.

* [A]   8°-From among brethren directly assigned to houses under the immediate jurisdiction of the Master of the Order, two delegates if they total less than one hundred, three delegates if they total one hundred or more, chosen according to the norm of # 407-bis.

§ II.–In transacting business after the election of the Master:

1°- 2° (as in the text)

3° all those mentioned in I, 2° – 8° 6°.

239. (Techn.)

407-bis. Ord.–For the election of delegates going to an elective General Chapter, ~~houses~~ *convents* under the immediate jurisdiction of the Master of the Order are to be joined among themselves by the general council so as to form two or three elective colleges, depending on the number of delegates to be elected. Each college must have at least twenty-five vocals. The same general council will provide for the manner of conducting this election.

240.

* [A]   407-bis. Ord.-For the election of delegates going to an elective General Chapter, brethren of houses under the immediate jurisdiction of the Master of the Order are to be joined among themselves by the general council so as to form two or three elective colleges, depending on the number of delegates to be elected. Each college must have

~~at least twenty-five vocals. The same general council will provide for the manner of conducting this election.~~

241. (Techn.)

408. Const.–The following are assembled and have voice in a General Chapter of Diffinitors:
1° –5°
6° One delegate from among the brethren assigned to ~~houses~~ *convents* under the immediate jurisdiction of the Master of the Order if the total is less than one hundred, two if the total is one hundred or more, elected according to the norm of LCO 409-ter.

242. (R 280)

408. Const.–The following are assembled and have voice in a General Chapter of Diffinitors:
1°–3° (as in the texts)

** [A] 4° delegates elected from each Vice Province ~~and general vicariate;~~

243.

408. Const.–The following are assembled and have voice in a General Chapter of Diffinitors:
1°–3° (as in the text)
4° (as in the text with a change introduced by the previous number)

* [A] ~~5° delegates of other vicariates, chosen in accord with n.409 bis, excluding, however, regional priors and Vicars Provincial;~~

* [A] ~~6° one delegate from among the brethren assigned to houses under the immediate jurisdiction of the Master of the Order if the total is less than one hundred, two if the total is one hundred or more, elected according to the norm of LCO 409-ter;~~

85

244. (R 281)

> 409. The following are assembled and have voice in a General Chapter of priors provincial:
> 1°–3°(as in the text)

** [A]   4° each Vice Provincial ~~and vicar generals~~;

245.

> 409. Const.–The following are assembled and have voice in a General Chapter of priors provincial:
> 1°–3°(as in the text)
> 4° (as in the text with a change introduced by the previous number)

* [A]   5° ~~delegates of the vicariates chosen from regional priors and Vicars Provincial in accord with n.409 bis.~~

* [A]   6° ~~one delegate from among the brethren assigned to houses under the immediate jurisdiction of the Master of the Order if the total is less than one hundred, two if the total is one hundred or more, elected according to the norm of LCO 409-ter.~~

246. (Techn.)

> 409-bis. Const.–Each Province which has at least twenty-five brothers assigned in ~~vicariates~~ *convents of the vicariates* or ~~houses~~ *convents* of their Province outside the boundaries of the Province has the right to send one delegate [...]

247. (R 282)

** [O]   409-bis. Const.–Each Province which has at least twenty-*five* brothers assigned in vicariates or houses of the Province outside the boundaries of the Province has the right to send one delegate [...]

248.

* [A]   409-bis. Const.–Each Province which has at least twenty-five   brothers assigned in vicariates or houses of the

Province outside the boundaries of the Province has the right to send one delegate elected from and by those brothers according to the statute of the Province to a General Chapter either of Diffinitors or priors provincial. (cf. appendix 17) A special arrangement shall be made by the Master of the Order with his council so that half of the Provinces shall be represented in one chapter and the other half in the next.

249. (Techn.)

409-ter. Const.–For the election of delegates going to a General Chapter of Diffinitors or priors provincial, all the brethren of the ~~houses~~ *convents* under the immediate jurisdiction of the Master of the Order are to be gathered among themselves by the general council [...]

250.

* [A]   409-ter. Const.–~~For the election of delegates going to a General Chapter of Diffinitors or priors provincial, all the brethren of the houses under the immediate jurisdiction of the Master of the Order are to be gathered among themselves by the general council to constitute elective colleges Each of these colleges should have at least twenty-five vocals. The general council will provide for the way in which this election is conducted.~~

251. (Techn.)

433. Ord.–Every brother shall conduct the special business of a ~~house~~ *convent* or Province with the Holy See through the mediation of the procurator of the Order whose competency it is to provide this service, [...]

252.

◆   434. The postulator general *for causes of beatification and canonization:*

1° discharges his office according to the norms established by the Holy See and the statute approved by the Master of the Order;

2° *at least once a year renders an account in writing to the Master General on the financial status, in which monies received, expenses, and a balance of credits and debits is described;*

2°3° gives reports to each General Chapter on the state of each cause.

253. (R 283)

✦✦ [A] 452. Ord.–In the actual election of superiors, this is the procedure:
1°-6° (as in the text)
7. the tellers and then the vocals ~~beginning from the older~~, one by one place their folded ballots in an open container;
8°-16° (as in the text)

254. (Techn.)

465. Ord.–The election of a conventual prior needs the confirmation of the Prior Provincial or of the regional prior if this concerns a brother assigned to a ~~regional vicariate~~ *convent of the regional vicariate* and elected for a convent in the same vicariate unless the statutes of the vicariate provide otherwise. (cf. appendix n. 20).

255. (R 284)

** [A] 465. Ord.–The election of a conventual prior needs the confirmation of the Prior Provincial ~~or of the regional prior if this concerns a brother assigned to a convent of the regional vicariate and elected for a convent in the same vicariate unless the statutes of the vicariate provide otherwise.~~ (cf. appendix n. 20).

256. (Techn.)

> 478. Ord.–The electors are the brothers enjoying active voice who are assigned to the ~~vicariate~~ *convents of the vicariate* directly or indirectly by reason of office.

257. (R 285)

** [A]   481. Const. ~~§ I. – For the confirmation or cassation of the election of a regional prior and his acceptance, nn. 465-473 shall be observed.~~
~~§ II.–The right of appointing a regional prior reverts to the Prior Provincial, n.373,1, being observed:~~
~~1° when at the time of the vacancy in the office of regional prior, the vicariate does not have the conditions stated in n.384; then, however, nn. 483 and 484 must be observed in the appointment of a vicar;~~
~~2° when all the vocals shall have renounced their voice and shall not have been reinstated by the Prior Provincial;~~
~~3° when for any reason whatsoever a regional prior has not been elected or postulated within six months of the known vacancy;~~
~~4° when in the process of election there have been seven futile scrutinies (cf. n.480, II, 2);~~
~~5° when the brethren elect the same brother again after the first election has been cassated, unless that election was cassated only because of procedural form and not because of the character of the one elected;~~
~~6° when there have been two or at most three elections confirmed by the Prior Provincial and not accepted by those elected; then after the second election the Prior Provincial can, and, after the third he must, appoint a regional prior.~~

258. (R 286)

** [A]   482. Const.–~~What has been established in nn. 477-481 for the election of a regional prior applies also, with appropriate modifications, to the election of a Vicar Provincial (see n.389).~~

259. (R 287)

** [A]   483. Const.–~~When a Vicar Provincial must be appointed by the Prior Provincial, the brethren, who in accord with n.478 would have active voice in the election, shall first be consulted (see Appendix n. 24).~~

260.

* [A]   497. Const.–§ I.–While observing n.491, § II, and with the exception of those who according to the norm of number 352, I, 6 and III are already represented the following elect a delegate to a Provincial Chapter, provided they enjoy active voice (see nn. 440 and 441):
      1° (as in the text);
      2° ~~unless it is indicated otherwise in the statute of the Province,~~ brothers directly assigned to houses or convents under the immediate jurisdiction of the Master of the Order, excepting always those who belong to the general council;
      3°–4° (as in the text)

261. (Techn.)

499.–§ I.–It pertains to the provincial council or to the regional council to determine for each elective college whether the vocals must meet in special session to hold the election or vote by mail.
§ II. If the election is to be held in a special assembly:
1° (as in the text);
2° in the very act of election, nn. 452 and 494, § ~~III~~ *IV;* shall be observed;
3° (as in the text).

262.

✦ [A]   499. Ord.–§ I.–It pertains to the provincial council ~~or to the regional council~~ to determine for each elective college whether the vocals must meet in special session to hold the election or vote by mail.
      § II. If the election is to be held in a special assembly:

1° the president (praeses) and place of the election shall be determined by the provincial ~~or regional~~ council;

2° (as in the text with the technical change)

3° (as in the text).

§ III.–If, however, the vocals cannot gather together conveniently:

1° each vocal shall write his vote on a ballot and send it in a double envelope to the Prior Provincial ~~or regional prior~~ in accord with n.480, III;

2°–3° (as in the text).

4° if, however, an absolute majority is not obtained in the first scrutiny, the Prior Provincial ~~or regional prior~~ with his council shall proceed according to the norms of n.480, IV, 6°, and 7°. In the final scrutiny, whether it is the second (n. 6°), third or fourth (n. 7°), only those two can be presented who achieved the greater number of votes, with number 450, III remaining in force.

263. (R 288)

◆ ◆ 499. Ord.–§ III.–If, however, the vocals cannot gather together conveniently, it takes place according to the following norms:

1° (as in the text with the change introduced in the preceeding number)

2° when the time determined for the reception of ballots has elapsed, the Prior Provincial or the regional prior with his council *or with two secretaries approved by the council* shall make the scrutiny in accord with n.480, IV, 1°–4°;

3° (as in the text).

4° (as in the text with the change introduced in the preceeding number)

264. (Techn.)

522. To be capable of being elected a Diffinitor of a General Chapter or a socius of a Diffinitor or of a Prior Provincial, it is required that:

[...]

3° That he not be directly assigned in ~~houses~~ *convents* under the immediate jurisdiction of the Master of the Order.

265. (Techn.)

567. Ord.–1° Annual financial report, that is, a complete statement on the economic state of each of its entities. In it are written the monies received, expenses, an account of debits and credits, a budget estimate for the following year as well as plans begun or about to be. If however the entity has several *convents or* houses or institutes, the same must be done for each. […]

266. (Techn.)

598. Const.–Needed money shall be given by their superior to the brethren when traveling. After the completion of the journey they shall give him a report on that money and any other received while outside the ~~house~~ *convent.*

267. (Techn.)

[For Appendices LCO]
Letters of Assignment (LCO 271 § ~~III~~)
Text to be inserted before the actual text:
13.A Form of direct ordinary assignment

268.

[For Appendices LCO]
13.B   Form of direct Assignment by reason of the Agreement of Priors Provincials (According to the Form of the G. C. of Providence)

I, Brother N.N., Prior Provincial of the Province *of A,*
to our beloved Brother N, son of the Province *of B.*
Considering the needs of the Order and your ability in the service of Christ, by tenor of the present document, and by my authority of Office, with the consent of the Prior Provincial of the Province of BBB, by virtue of LCO 391, 6°, revoking your prior

assignment from the Convent in which you are at present assigned, I assign you by reason of the agreement between Provinces, to the Convent of St. Nnn, (or to the house of St. N), Nnnnn, for such a time (for the designated time of studies by the Prior Provincial of the aforesaid Province, for the academic year, for two years, for three years, for four years, for five years), *commanding you in virtue of holy obedience and under formal precept, that within so many days you undertake a journey there, and you transfer yourself to the said convent (or to the said house), and* I direct the superior of the aforesaid convent (or house) to receive you kindly and treat you charitably, as legitimately assigned.

Following the norm of n. 391, 6° LCO, and according to the declaration laid down in the appendix n. 16 in the LCO, as well as the agreement stipulated between priors provincials, you have the obligations and the rights of any of the friars in this convent, except active and passive voice with respect to the election for the Provincial Chapter of Province A, keeping however active and passive voice for electing a delegate going to the Provincial Chapter of your Province B.

Given at N(city or town), in the Convent of N, under the seal of the Province, on the N day of the month of N, in the year of our Lord NNN.

Whatsoever to the contrary, notwithstanding.

(seal of the Province)   Brother N, O.P.
                                                         Prior Provincial
Reg. pag.
Brother N, O.P.
Secretary

269.

[For Appendices LCO]
13.C Form of Indirect Assignment

I, Brother N, O.P. Prior Provincial of the Province *of A*,
to our beloved Brother N, son of the Province *of B*

Considering the needs of the Order and your ability in the service of Christ, by tenor of the present document, and by my authority of Office, revoking your prior assignment from the Convent in which you are at present assigned, I assign you by reason of studies, to the Convent of St. N (or to the house of St. N) Nnnn, for the time of studies designated by the Prior Provincial of the aforesaid Province, (for the academic year, for two years, for three years, for four years, for five years), commanding you in virtue of holy obedience and under formal precept, that within so many days you undertake a journey there, and you transfer yourself by direct route to the said convent (or to the said house), and I direct the superior of the aforesaid convent (or house) to receive you kindly and treat you charitably, as legitimately assigned. You have the obligaitons and rights, by reason of the stipulations signed by the two Prior Provincials

OR:

Following the norm of n. 270 § III LCO, unless it is warned otherwise in the agreement, the obligations of each of the brothers and rights you have, especially to participate in the chapters and community meetings, and the common life and celebration of the liturgy. Keeping always n. 208 LCO, as well as the agreement stipulated between priors provincials, you have the obligations and the rights of any of the friars in this convent, except active and passive voice with respect to 208 LCO, you enjoy active voice in the conventual chapter except for elections and financial matters.

For the planning of studies, you should refer to the regent of studies of the Province of your assignment. The time of this indirect assignment having expired, the direct assignment revives, or simply the one previously done.

Given at N(city or town), in the Convent of N, under the seal of the Province, on the N day of the month of N, in the year of our Lord NNN.

Whatsoever to the contrary, notwithstanding.

(seal of the Province)   Brother N, O.P.
                                                                        Prior Provincial

Reg. pag.
Brother N, O.P.
Secretary

270.

[For Appendices LCO]
14-bis. On the vote of Superiors in Council (LCO 297-bis)

From an authentic response of the Pontifical Commision for interpretation of the Code of Canon Law: "On the superior and his council" (July 5, 1985, AAS, 1985, p. 771), not a few doubts have arisen, about which the General Chapter of Dublin in 1986, (Acta, N. 151) has acted.

Now already the matter is somewhat clarified because both the teaching of reputable authors, and the recent praxis of the Roman Curia, maintain that Religious Institutes are able to fix the norms to be followed regarding their own Councils by the authority of the autonomy of their Institutes (Cf. Can. 627)

After the matter was promptly considered by our General Council, the Master General presiding, and having heard other experts in Canon Law, the following conclusion has been arrived at:

Superiors of our Order, whether brothers or nuns, following our proper Constitutions as they have been interpreted by immemorial custom, can cast a vote together with their Council.

Given at Rome, by order of the Master of the Order and his Council, February 17, 1988.

Fr. Raphael Moya, O.P.
Procurator General
[*Analecta* 96 (1988), 188-189]

271. (Techn.)

[For Appendices LCO]
19. On habitual residence (450 § I)

From the Acts of the General Chapter celebrated at Tallaght in 1971 (n.159):

We declare that the term habitual residence must refer to the residence which a brother has in any place by reason of employment and for a period of time which is extended longer than in the ~~house~~ *convent* of his assignment [...]

272. *[Commemoration]* We remind the General Curia of the Order of the Commission of ACG 2010 Rome n. 297 regarding the publication on the official website of the Order of an *editio typica* of the LCO and a list of ordinations of the General Chapters not included in the LCO, yet in force.

273. *[Commemoration]* We remind the General Curia of the Order of the Commission of ACG 2010 Rome n. 298 regarding a list of ordinations in force that should be reviewed by the Chapter Commission whose material corresponds to its competence.

274. *[Commission]* We commission the Master of the Order that, in preparation of the next General Chapter, the General Curia study all those numbers of the LCO regarding "assignations" (nn. 270 and 271; 391, 6° and the *Declaratio* in *Appendix 16* LCO, ed. 2010).

275. *[Thanksgiving]* We thank the *ad hoc* commission, consisting of brothers Angelo Urru, Javier Pose, and Konštanc Adam, under the presidency of brother Philippe Toxé, procurator general of the Order, appointed by the Master to review our Constitutions, for the great service they have rendered to this Chapter through their careful work on desirable modifications to our Constitutions. The work of several of the chapter commissions would have been difficult or impossible without this preparation.

Thanksgivings

276. The General Chapter of Trogir expresses its warmest gratitude to all who contributed to the preparation and successful outcome of the Chapter, namely:
- the Province of Croatia, which hosted the chapter,
- those assigned to simultaneous translation and translation of texts, those who prepared liturgies, those who wrote the

minutes, and all others who according to their particular functions greatly assisted the chapter
- the staff of Hotel Sveti Križ, Arbanija, who took such good care of us.

Site of the Next General Chapter

We declare that the next General Chapter, which will be of Prior Provincials, will be celebrated in the convent of our Holy Father Saint Dominic at Bologna, during the summer months of 2016, the exact date to be fixed later.

Suffrages for the Living

- For Pope Francis, Supreme Pastor of the Church and most benevolent benefactor of our Order, each Province shall celebrate one Mass.
- For Pope Emeritus Benedict XVI, each Province shall celebrate one Mass.
- For fr. Bruno Cadoré, Master of the Order, each Province shall celebrate one Mass.
- For fr. Timothy Radcliffe and fr. Carlos A. Azpiroz Costa, ex-Masters of the Order, each Province shall celebrate one Mass.
- For the entire Episcopal Order, for the *socii* of the Master of the Order, for the Procurator General of the Order, for our benefactors and for the well-being of the entire Order of Preachers, each Province shall celebrate one Mass.

Suffrages for the Dead

- For the soul of Pope John Paul I each Province shall celebrate one Mass.
- For the soul of fr. Damian Byrne, the most recently deceased Master of the Order, each Province shall celebrate one Mass.
- For the souls of the brothers and sisters of the Order who have died since the last General Chapter, each Province should celebrate one solemn Mass for them all together.

When these prescribed suffrages, for either the living or the dead are to be fulfilled, they should be announced publicly and in sufficient time, so that the brethren of the convent where the suffrages are to be fulfilled can participate in the Mass celebrated for these intentions.

These are the Acts of the General Chapter of Diffinitors, of Trogir in Croatia, celebrated in the convent of the Holy Cross on the island of Čiovo, from July 22 to August 8, 2013, of which the printed versions, fixed with the seal of the Master General, ought to be held with the same faith as the original text.

We command the superiors of all and each of the Provinces, convents and houses that the same acts be read as soon as possible in each of the convents and houses subject to them and to be published, and they should sedulously take care that they be observed by all.

In the name of the Father, and of the Son, and of the Holy Spirit.

Given in Trogir, in the convent of the Holy Cross, on the island of Čiovo, August 8, in the year of our Lord 2013.

L. ✠ S.

fr. Bruno Cadoré, OP
magister Ordinis

fr. Augustin Laffay, OP
diffinitor provinciæ Tolosanæ

fr. Juan Manuel Almarza Meñica, OP
diffinitor provinciæ Hispaniæ

fr. Anastazio Perica Petrić, OP
diffinitor provinciæ Croaticæ

fr. Mihael Mario Tolj, OP
secretarius generalis capituli

fr. Srećko Koralija, OP
ab actis

fr. Ivan Dominik Iličić, OP
ab actis

fr. Mirko Irenej Vlk, OP
ab actis

APPENDIX I

Relatio de statu Ordinis
to the General Chapter of Trogir (2013)

INTRODUCTION

1. In conformity with LCO 417 § II, 3°, I present my *Relatio de statu Ordinis* to the General Chapter of Diffinitors to be celebrated at Trogir (Croatia) from 22 July to 8 August 2013. Two perspectives guide my report: that of the celebration of the Jubilee of the Order in 2016, in which I am in continuity with the *Relatio* of Brother Carlos Azpiroz Costa to the General Chapter of Rome; and that of the orientations and questions expressed by that last General Chapter, which have guided the work of the General Council during the past three years.

2. The *socii* of the Master of the Order, the general promoters, and other officials of the general curia have presented their individual reports and these are to be taken as going together with the present *Relatio*. As well as that, the reports of the Prior Provincials and vicars general prepared with a view to the chapter give us all a knowledge of the reality of the Order, of the vitality of preaching, and of the principal challenges to be faced here and there. Introducing my own report gives me the opportunity to express my deep gratitude for the fraternity, support and collaboration of my *socii*, of the Curia as a whole, of the community of Santa Sabina, and of the Prior Provincials and vicars, as well as for the confidence of the brothers and sisters of the Order on which I have been able to rely from the beginning of my mandate.

3. The Acts of the Chapter of Rome begin with a unique Prologue dedicated to the ministry of preaching. This choice underlines our determination to use well the years between now and 2016 to renew our vocation, our life, and our mission as preachers. It seems to me that this dynamic ought to be followed, particularly at a time when the Church invites us to a profound renewal of evangelization, for

which the Order was specifically founded. I think therefore, that we ought resolutely to engage all our energy, and at all levels (personal, communitarian, provincial or vicarial general), in this movement, affirming and fulfilling our "office" of preachers *in medio Ecclesiae*. It is in this sense that a program for the celebration of the Jubilee is submitted for the approval of the General Chapter, with a view to engaging the Order in the same dynamic.

4. In writing this *Relatio* I have drawn a lot on my experience of visitations, meetings, and exchanges with the brothers during these three years. I would like it to be an occasion for all of us to give thanks for the beautiful reality of our preaching, and to give an echo to the questions and aspirations for the future which arise from this reality. May these pages contribute to the celebration of the Jubilee of the Order as an opportunity for participating in the renewal of evangelization and for strengthening our vocation as preachers.

Demography

5. Regarding the brothers, the statistics of the Order in 2012 show that we are at present 5,955 brothers, of whom 345 are cooperator brothers, 4,430 are priests, 918 are student brothers, 18 brothers are deacons, 208 novices and 36 bishops. Among these brothers one ought to note that 333 live *extra conventum* and that 84 are exclaustrated. In the course of the year 51 simply professed and 8 solemnly professed brothers asked to leave the Order, 19 asked to be dispensed from the priesthood. In one year, 109 brothers died.

On the basis of these figures several remarks can be made:

6. One brother in six is at present in initial formation, across all the regions of the Order, and it is a reason for gratitude at the same time as it is a great responsibility: more than ever initial formation ought to be for us a priority.

7. 7% of the brothers live outside community, and it seems to me that we ought to question ourselves about this fact and seek to remedy it. At the same time, we must not give up searching for the reasons which lead brothers to quit the

Order, in particular to ask for exclaustration in order to join the diocesan clergy. The accompaniment of brothers in difficult situations is essential, but it varies greatly from province to province.

8. Behind these figures, we ought also to recall that, in certain provinces, the average age is very high, something which invites us, at one and the same time, to take account of this fact of aging (both for the evangelical and apostolic challenge it represents as for the quality of accompaniment necessary in this phase of life), and to deploy an appropriate promotion of vocations.

9. Even if certain entities have the joy of new vocations to the cooperator brotherhood, the number of such brothers is proportionately weak, in spite of the importance of this specific vocation for the vocation of the Order, especially at a time when the mission of lay people is particularly valued in the Church.

10. Another fact revealed by these figures is the international reality of the Order and the intercultural character of many provinces and communities. The Order must appreciate that it is no longer primarily northwestern, and that the realities experienced in Western Europe and North America cannot by themselves constitute the paradigm for the deployment of our charism. Because the Order is already, like the world, constiuted by different cultures (with, perhaps, the wounded memory of cultural confrontations), and is established in different ecclesial histories and cultures, we must take particular care that no temptation to cultural, national or ecclesial *identitarianismes* or particularisms becomes an obstacle to our vocation to unity in heart and soul.

11. One ought to note here certain figures that indicate the extent of the Dominican family. As regards the nuns, there are 2,773 professed sisters, in 219 monasteries. There are 8 federations, 2 associations and one fraternal union.

There are in the Order about 150,000 Lay Dominicans and 16,000 associated lay people, 265 members of priestly fraternities (in 13 groups), 150 members of Dominican secular institutes, 24,296 apostolic Dominican sisters belonging to 150 congregations.

A first overview

12. During the first three years of my mandate I have been able to visit many provinces and vicariates of the Order, either in the initial round of rapid visits made in the first year in order to gain a first knowledge of the Order, or after that on the occasion of canonical visitations (Toulouse, Hungary, Poland, Croatia, Portugal, Netherlands, Mexico, Colombia, Ecuador, Chile, Province of the Most Holy Rosary, Flanders, Argentina, Canada, Holy Name of Jesus (USA), Upper Germany and Austria, Australia and New Zealand, South Belgium, Philippines, St Martin de Porres (USA), Pakistan, Central America, DR Congo, the Baltic countries, Russia and Ukraine, Puerto Rico, West Africa, Dominican Republic, Slovenia, the Vicariate of South America, Angola, Cuba, Japan, St. Stephen's in Jerusalem). Other canonical visitations have been carried out by the *socii*: France (with its vicariates), West Indies, Trinidad, Venezuela, Kenya, Rwanda and Burundi, the communities of St Dominic and St. Sixtus in Rome and of St. Albert in Fribourg.

13. In the course of these visits it has been a deep joy to discover *the vitality of an Order which preaches in great diversity*, cultural, ecclesial, and socio-political. "The brothers work and preach," one often hears it said, and this reality calls for gratitude.

14. I can witness to the happiness and gratitude which the vast majority of brothers express regarding their life in the Order and regarding their mission. They are happy to welcome new vocations, to transmit to younger brothers the tradition and history of the Order and of their province, and to strive to sustain their enthusiasm and their creativity.

15. I can witness also to *the often expressed regard on the part of protagonists in the local Churches* for the mission

realized by the brothers, within the perspectives of the challenges posed for evangelization today.

16. In spite of the difficulties and the insecurity implied in the demand of the last General Chapter that we work for a *restructuring of the most fragile entities*, I can confirm that the great majority of the brothers concerned acknowledge the sound basis for this and are disposed to engage in that work, understanding that what it is about is finding the best balance between the structures of fraternal life and the mission.

17. In many places the brothers are *thankful and proud of what we older ones have achieved*, while being determined not to live on the memory of past glories (which might cause us to run the risk of unjustified pride, or of relaxing into a tranquil good conscience), but rather to deploy humbly our present capacities.

18. Above all, if I may be permitted to write it, the visits have also been marked by the bright revelation of the mystery of each person in his life as a believer, of the fidelty of Christ accompanying each one on his way. Brother Timothy spoke of a *"pilgrimage in the Order,"* and it is probably the most profound experience which it has been given me to have.

19. Each entity, because of its culture and its history, is certainly faced with specific challenges and difficulties. Many questions are, however, common, and express the desire to *see, without nourishing ourselves with false hopes, what ways are best adapted for deploying our "office of preaching."*

20. In the context of important changes in the world, and of its globalization, which entails a great interdependence of all but also the coexistence of many contemporary worlds in the same place, the insistence of the Church on a *renewal of evangelization is an appeal to all to renew and adapt the manner in which the proper charism of the Order is deployed.* This appeal is experienced as greatly stimulating by most of us, but at the same time there are difficulties and resistances

that cannot be ignored: we are often very set in apostolic involvements and positions which it is not easy to shift; the "overwork" of many often prevents us taking the time for evaluation and for adaptation to social and ecclesial changes; the very "individualistic" directions of preaching (in the largest possible sense, including also teaching and research) of each one does not facilitate a reflection on our common apostolic responsibility, to which the great difficulties in formulating communitarian or provincial projects that would define the criteria for prioritizing, that we all assume, testify; the link between apostolic work and economic resources (and so the level of life we have established, often very demanding) easily leads to fear of losing that which we consider a security. There is here, I think, the need to allow ourselves to be questioned again by *the double choice by Dominic of itinerancy and mendicancy. It is at this price that we must undertake the innovations and new foundations that are necessary today.*

21. *Two fundamental preoccupations about the mission of preaching* are particularly stressed by the brothers, even though we do not always know how to respond well. The first is the question of *leaving our established positions in order to go instead to encounter people* who no longer come to our convents or to our churches. There is the concern about those who quit the Catholic Church for different reasons, without knowing how one might best accompany them so that they might feel at home in the Church. There is the concern about those who have never encountered the Gospel, in particular the younger generations. There is the concern about the encounter of contemporary cultures and knowledge with which the tradition of the Order urges us to enter into dialogue. *The second preoccupation is about those "forgotten by the world"* whose voice hardly counts at all in the culture that actually dominates. Yes, in many ways, we affirm the necessity of struggling against poverty and injustices, the importance of giving a priority to the consideration of serious contemporary problems such as social marginalization, forced migrations, the absence of respect for and the promotion of the rights of entire populations: we ought

to note well that our common endeavours in these areas remain very exceptional and marginal. Briefly, the two "cries of Dominic" which brother Vincent de Couesnongle liked to cite–*"never without the poor." "never without the furthest away"* – can remain also for us actual appeals and can determine our preaching of the covenant of the friendship of God with human beings.

22. Very often, in the course of visitations, we have spoken with the brothers about the intuition of Dominic in founding the Order not only to "manage" the ecclesial reality of the time, but rather *to contribute to the renewal of the Church*– having, as Dominic did, an urgent concern to promote its unity – *the dialogue of the Gospel with new human, social, religious, spiritual and ecclesial realities*, as also with the many traditions of thought and with new forms of knowledge. Too often, perhaps, we think of our mission today in terms of ministries established within the structural functioning of the Church. It is, undoubtedly, important, and the work achieved by the brothers wins our admiration. But how are we to be "displaced" by new needs, in fidelity to our own proper tradition? What might be the specific services, inspired by the tradition of the Order, which the Dominican friars of today can bring to the Church, faced with the changes in the world which, in many ways, seem analogous to those at the moment of our foundation?

23. There is no shortage of demands addressed to the Order *to respond to new needs*. I have noticed many times that our first reflex tends to be to evaluate the weakness of our resources or the absence of a formation appropriate for such needs, and this leads us to decline the invitation. It seems to me that, in certain situations, it would be more fitting to take the time and the means to form the brothers who could then dedicate themselves to these new apostolic fields, accepting that it will mean abandoning other engagements that are less important.

24. It is striking to recall that Dominic's proposal was not to enunciate a "program of action," but more the proposal of a

"way of life and encounter," inviting his brothers to live in fraternal communities as evangelical and apostolic men, contemplatives and preachers. *Preachers, because contemplatives.* In many places, the friars acknowledge the necessity of drawing anew from this source, to recover the air of a "mysticism of the life of the preacher," to avoid dissipating or losing ourselves in an apostolic activism which would relegate to a place of less importance the fraternal life, the common celebration of the Word in the Office and in the community Eucharist, and contemplative study. This is to say that the aspiration of many is to draw from the tradition of the Order a strengthening in the culture of evangelical communion which will carry each and all in his apostolic vocation.

25. Initial formation is a major task for the great majority of the provinces and for the Order as a whole. It is really an immense grace that we are receiving new brothers: their generosity, what it is they dream of achieving as preachers in a world in profound change, the "worlds" and the "cultures" which they bring with them to the Order, as well as their calls to witness to the friendship of God with humanity and the announcing of the Gospel. All of this ought to stimulate our common apostolic creativity. How are we to open with them ways for this generosity to find its full realization, without the long but necessary years of initial formation and institutional study stifling the flame? What ought to be the specificity of formation and studies for this? What is the specific service of the Church for which we think the Order has the duty to prepare them? How can we propose to them studies which are not just those that meet the requirements of priestly ministry? How are we to deploy well the promotion of vocations (some provinces really neglect this aspect too much), without forgetting the promotion of the vocation of the cooperator brother at a time in the Church when there is a call to strengthen the lay ministry of evangelization? All of these questions occupy the many superiors and masters of formation in the Order but they ought to be carried by the friars as a whole. It is important, for example, that everyone shares a common attachment to the life in

which the young are being formed. In certain places, the development of collaborations seems indispensable in order not to exhaust the energies of some brothers.

26. *To study, to preach, and to found convents.* So, it is said, Dominic sent the first friars, a little uncertain at the thought of taking to the roads. Because, in the perspective of the Jubilee, we must reinforce the roots and the living out of our mission, I propose to follow these three "sendings" in composing the rest of this *Relatio.*

TO STUDY

27. *To study and contemplate the truth*: this essential dimension of the mission of the Order represents an important part of the reality of the brothers' work today. Even more, it is particularly required in the current perspective of evangelization. Pope Benedict XVI expressed the expectation which the Church has of us in regard to evangelization by underlining the opportunity the tradition of the Order gives us of holding together "study and adoration." Preaching also sends us back to the need for study, rooted in the human adventure, intellectual and spiritual, for the twofold encounter with God and with our contemporaries. At a time when the heart and the reason are very often constrained to be disconnected, *the tradition of contemplative study is perhaps one of the primary services of freedom which* we can offer to our contemporaries.

Priority of the life of study in the Order

28. The Chapter of Rome (in continuity with the preceding chapters) articulated numerous questions and orientations concerning the life of study in the Order. The report of the *socius* for the life of study gives an account of the responses given to these questions and the processes that are underway. I stress four points for your attention:

29. The composition of the *permanent commission for the promotion of studies in the Order* was modified to include representatives of the Regents. This implies a "mobility" in the shape of the commission that needs to be evaluated. But

it establishes also the advantage of inscribing the concern for study more deeply in the heart of the life of the provinces and of encouraging collaborations, exchanges and synergies. This aspect seems important to me since, on many occasions during the course of my first visitations, the brothers have remarked that study seems to hold a very modest place in the habitual life of our entities and that we often, as a result, neglect the exigencies of the life of study that have marked the Order during the past decades and so also the capacities for expertise which we would still be willing work for. If this fact is confirmed, it is essential to maintain the effort to affirm the essential place of study in the life and mission of the Order (LCO 83). To promote the *"culture of study"* among us, besides an indispensable revaluation of the role of the conventual lector, the following three points ought to sustain our efforts.

30. The work of evaluating the various *centers of study and research* in the Order is under way. It brings to light not only the importance given to study in the provinces and the number of brothers who are dedicated to it, not only the necessity (in fact with restricted human resources) but also the interest, on the basis of these evaluations, of promoting collaborations and synergies as regards teaching, research and institutional studies during initial formation. It seems important also to be careful that the concern about organizing a center for initial studies does not prevent us from developing other projects of study and research, not strictly connected with initial academic teaching: both are precious for the vitality of a province. This is why, in order to avoid dissipating our forces and to promote well the poten-tiality and specificity of the mission of study and research in the Order, it seems to me that we ought to explore how to organize well the complementarity among our institutions, something that will favor at one and the same time the quality of initial study, a common culture of study shared in by the students belonging to many entities, collaboration between teachers and researchers, and the availability of these latter for research and publication which are so impor-tant for the life of the Church today. One knows how the links

established between the brothers through study and research were important for the remarkable contribution of our brother-theologians during the Second Vatican Council. These synergies are certainly very important at a time when study ought to be the place of *interdisciplinary dialogue between theology and the many new forms of knowledge.*

31. A revision of the *Ratio studiorum* is being prepared and a first outline will be presented at the chapter. This ought to be the occasion to affirm once again the importance of institutional studies in initial formation as well as of complementary studies asked of the new brothers with a view not only to their gifts but also to the needs of the service the Order can offer to the Church. It seems to me that we must insist here on the fact that we ought to guide the brothers in formation through a course of demanding studies whose goal is not limited to obtaining the grades necessary for ordination to ministries, but which seeks to anchor study at the heart of the process of integrating the person of the preacher. The actual evolution of the norms for institutional studies tends to increase demands of an academic kind (hours of teaching, content of programs to be realized, evaluations). Generally the new friars join the Order with great enthusiasm for study and for the search for truth, carrying with them the questions of the world from which they come: how are we to welcome, maintain and develop this enthusiasm? We must be careful that this does not endanger the disposition of the student brothers to attain, beyond grades and qualifications, a true *habitus* of study. Whether they study at centers of the Order or at the university, we have the responsibility to ask them to give *an absolute priority to study during the time of initial formation*, giving them the taste for a "free" and contemplative study: assiduous study of the Bible, solid philosophical formation, rigorous knowledge of Thomist thought and of its inherent capacity for dialogue with other systems of thought, reading the great philosophical and theological authors, working for a critical knowledge of the sources, exigent dialogue with contemporary forms of knowledge. Here or there, I have noticed a tendency to privilege profane formation (certainly

important for dialogue with contemporary forms of knowledge) over deeper studies in theology, and I think this risks, in the medium term, weakening the theological service of the Order. Defining the objectives, demands and methods of study in this way, as a whole, and according to the tradition of the Order, this theological service of the Order needs to be safeguarded from the arbitrariness of subjective choices or ideologies, so as to constitute in reality a privileged way of service which the Order wishes to offer to the Church. In re-affirming the place of study in initial formation, we must think particularly of regions of the Order where it is very difficult to manage study because of the sociopolitical context or economic constraints. It is a priority for the culture of solidarity which we want to promote in the Order.

32. Along with the General Council, we have redefined the process for promotion to the grade of *Master in Sacred Theology*, and we rejoice that a very large number of proposals have been presented by the provinces. I would like the body of Masters in Sacred Theology to be available to accompany the Order in its confrontation with the questions posed today in the field of theology, and to help us all in confronting them through our preaching. It seems to me that many themes preoccupy the brothers today both for the life of study in itself, as well as for the articulation between study and preaching: the place of the critical study of Thomas in theological formation; the consideration of other religions; a deeper knowledge of the orientations defined by the Second Vatican Council; the impact of this Council for a theology of the laity in the Church, and its consequences for the life of the Order (the ministries of the cooperator brothers, the ministries of the laity in the Order, of the apostolic sisters ...); the impact of the ecclesiology of Vatican II for the theology of the religious life and on the place of the religious life in the Church's mission of evangelization.

A culture of study and dialogue

33. From many points of view *we can rejoice in the reality of the life of study in the Order*, if we judge it by the great number of brothers involved in teaching and research in theology and in philosophy, by the different centers of specialized studies, and by the participation of many brothers in institutions of research and teaching external to the Order, and by the numerous publications. One ought to rejoice also in the attachment of a great number of brothers to study, quite apart from the academic dimension. It is often very impressive to hear the brothers speaking with passion about their reading and their study. One ought to note that many among the brothers in formation insist on the fact that this vocation of the Order to study and to the search for truth, has played an important part in their vocational decision. At the same time, one ought to say that renewed efforts need to be made if we want, realistically, to live up to the standard of this specific vocation.

34. I would like therefore to underline certain points to which, during the visitations, the brothers draw my attention, expressing their desire to insert study more, and concretely, in the heart of the life of the communities:

> 35. *Study ought to be inscribed in a habitual manner in the "culture" of each community*, thereby bringing its proper part to the constitution itself of the fraternal communion which unites us. Too often the brothers relate in the course of the visitations that this dimension of study has little place in the building up of the communities and that as regards study very little is expected of the conventual lector or of the promoter of continuing formation. How are we to understand and remedy such a deficit?
>
> 36. *A study together of the Word of God*, for example, ought to take a more central place in our communities. Some communities speak of the benefits they have received from this, in the form of a time of *lectio divina* in common, a sharing on the texts of the day as a way of preparing for preaching, a reading of things experienced in the light of

the Word. Is it not a practice that ought to be generalized, in the perspective of the celebration of the Jubilee of the confirmation of the Order as the Order of Preachers?

37. Many of us stress that the dimension of *dialogue and debate with the currents of contemporary thought, with the other religions, and with scientific and technical forms of knowledge* so rich in the world today, should constantly be promoted. In many ways, apostolic and pastoral engagements confront us with the complexity of the questions posed by economics, by the challenges to the rights of nations and peoples, to the anthropological impact of the globalized culture of the modern world, to the urgency of a real ecological vigilance. These questions, in the way that they impact on themes in ecclesiology, on the theology of the religious life, or on pastoral theology, evoke many of the challenges which evangelization must face today. I have often noticed, in the meetings of the communities, that even if these questions preoccupy all of us, we take little time to reflect seriously on them together. At a time when the need to renew the mission of evangelization is evident to everybody, I believe we ought to take concrete steps to give more space to such reflection in our communities and in our provinces. This would stimulate greatly our common apostolic responsibility and creativity, rooting them in theological work that is in dialogue with contemporary cultures and their challenges. It is the responsibility of the centers and institutions of study placed under the jurisdiction of the Master of the Order to open us to these arguments.

38. In many places one notices that there is *a certain distance between the theological or philosophical reflection undertaken by the brothers, and the pastoral experiences encountered in particularly difficult human, social and scientific contexts*, especially those where the rights of persons are gravely threatened. At the moment when we celebrated the memory of the famous sermon of Montesinos, and in the line traced by brothers such as Las Casas and Vitoria, I asked the Promoter for Justice and

Peace and the Delegate of the Order to the United Nations Organization, to manage a project called *"the Salamanca Process"* (in the Philippines, Colombia, and which will extend to other places such as Kiev, Chicago, and Yamoussoukro). It seeks to promote dialogue between theology and the profane sciences taught in certain of our universities, starting from a concrete confrontation with pastoral experience. The history of the development of the "right of peoples" by the School of Salamanca shows us the potential fruitfulness of such dialogues and the contribution they can make to the transformation of the world. We know well that today analogous challenges are not in short supply (in very different areas: political reality, the world of work, education, health...) and call theology more than ever to be a key part of evangelization, favoring interdisciplinary research beginning from the problems encountered in the pastoral domain. It is a demanding responsibility for the theological institutions which may, however, be tempted – in the name of a tradition they wish to defend but in fact are contradicting – to regard themselves as self-sufficient and to resist dialogue with other forms of knowledge and other experiences.

The academic Institutions under the immediate jurisdiction of the Master of the Order

39. The permanent commission for the life of study has also initiated a reflection concerning the institutions of study that are placed directly under the jurisdiction of the Master of the Order, of which the Chapter of Rome also demanded an evaluation. I would like here to underline some points:

40. The *ad hoc* Commission demanded by the chapter concerning *the University of Saint Thomas Aquinas at Manila* (ACG 2010 Rome 219) was established and, on the basis of its conclusions, I took the decision to complete the process initiated by the General Chapter of Caleruega and *to transfer the direct jurisdiction* of the University to the Province of the Philippines which has already in practice taken charge of it.

In fact the direct jurisdiction of the Master of the Order made sense as long as a convent depending directly on him was structurally tied to the University, but this is no longer the case. Taking account of the importance of this University, not just for the province but for the Order as a whole, it was decided that the Master of the Order would always be Grand Chancellor of this pontifical University. We have therefore defined in a precise way the organic links between the University and the province, as well as the mediations by which the Master of the Order exercises his responsibility as Chancellor. Proposals for modifications of the statutes were worked out by the commission and these will be presented for approval to the competent Dicastery.

41. As regards the other *institutions of study under the direct jurisdiction of the Master of the Order*, I took the initiative to bring together the brothers with responsibility in these different institutions. This resulted in a "Charter" which defines the specific service which these institutions can offer today, and could serve as a basis on which to imagine now the relationships of collaboration and synergy between these institutions, and between them and the provinces. One might highlight in particular what concerns the specific contribution of these institutions to the mission of the Order, the place they take in formation within the Church, the appreciation of their contribution in their scientific environment, the opportunity they represent for the formation of friars of different provinces and particularly for certain of their teams in the area of studies, as well as the conventions by which the contribution of the provinces to the teaching and research in these institutions can be prepared. Certain objectives have been reaffirmed to promote the development of these institutions:

o 42. Reflections undertaken in these institutions over many years show that we are at a crucial moment in preparing for the future, that there is a need to *"change the paradigm."* Whatever the reputation acquired over many decades and the actual quality of work accomplished, the enduring character of these institutions is no longer self-evident, because the landscape and the requirements of teaching and research in the Church as in the world have profoundly changed. It is a case now of *making precise once more the mission which the Order entrusts to these institutions*, and to put in place *new modalities of governance*, academic as well as economic and administrative, adapted to the contemporary context, taking account of the resources but also of the needs of the provinces, which will permit them to affirm the specificity of their contribution in the field of research and teaching in the Church. It is in this sense that a process of evaluation has been initiated with the École Biblique and the University of Saint Thomas in Rome.

o 43. Each of these institutions, responding to a precise need of the Order, ought to establish *with the provinces as a whole*, reciprocal relationships of familiarity, regard, confidence and service.

o 44. For each it is right to promote its just autonomy in relation to the Curia which has the task not only of helping to respond to their needs in terms of human resources and economic means, but also of assuring their good governance and of taking steps to evaluate regularly with the institution the response it is giving to the mission entrusted to it.

o 45. The character they have as "communities of study and research" ought to be privileged as specific to our tradition, something which requires particular care for supporting the life of these communities.

o 46. They ought to develop even more their links with analogous institutions of research and teaching, and to be concerned to give to teachers and researchers the practical necessities for their mission.

o 47. Priority is given to certain themes that are particularly entrusted to these institutions: study of the

Bible; critical knowledge of the Thomist tradition; the articulation between philosophy and theology; the capacity to bring theology into dialogue with the sciences and with contemporary currents of thought, an echo of discerning the signs of the times; the articulation between theology and preaching (or evangelization).

o 48. The objective for the next three years ought to be to strengthen and to renew the communities of teacher-researchers in these institutions, on the basis of new perspectives that emerge in the evaluations and are identified in the strategic plans already drawn up, this along with improved, perhaps radically new, conditions of economic management.

TO PREACH

49. In its Prologue, the Chapter of Rome wanted to place the entirety of its work under the sign of preaching. It made very clear the reality of the *office of preaching* – which in the Order takes so many, diverse, and wonderful forms – *to which the life of the friars preachers is totally consecrated*, in this way giving our religious life its specific form. The grace of the coming celebration of the Jubilee, as well as the appeal made to all religious institutes by the recent Synod on the new evangelization, invite us to live this consecration ever more fully and to actualize it ceaselessly.

50. This invites us also to place our reflection within the larger horizon of what might be the creativity in terms of preaching of the Dominican family as constituting somehow, since its foundation, what one calls nowadays a "spiritual family." How might we realistically give form to this reality which is defined precisely by the mission of evangelization?

Promoting reflection on the mission: apostolic creativity and "mobility"

51. In the section of the Acts dedicated to the ministry of the Word (ACG 2010 Rome 128-184), the Chapter of Rome identified a certain number of areas for which it encouraged the brothers to deepen their engagement and their reflection. The themes underlined were: presence to indigenous cultures, pastoral work in parishes, encountering movements of migration, dialogue with other religions, evangelization in the world of education, preaching in the new worlds of communication, schools of preaching, to which we have added pastoral involvement in popular devotions and pilgrimages, and city center pastoral work. To implement this demand of the chapter, we thought in the council that it would be a good opportunity to initiate a dialogue between the provinces on these matters. This is why I asked certain provinces, each one particularly involved in one of these apostolic fields, to present a first reflection on one of these themes, thus providing a first contribution to the reflection in which all might participate. This process was put in place last year and, since October 2012, the dialogue has been added progressively to the intranet site of the Order. Experience so far is hesitant but the present chapter can develop this reflection on the basis of the following elements.

52.   The themes brought forward by the Chapter of Rome link at once with *the priorities and frontiers* for the mission of the Order defined over many years in successive chapters, and with the main preoccupations of the Church concerning evangelization. It is why we have suggested to the Prior Provincials to give their attention to these themes in the reflections on the mission of evangelization that they will present to the chapter. This can be something to support the orientations and proposals which the chapter, if it judges it to be good, might formulate for the years to come, *helping each entity in this way to review its apostolic planning in the perspective of the Jubilee of the Order.*

53.   Promoting *apostolic dialogue* within the Order on all these subjects, as well as on those which are already the object of "networks" (media, pastoral work in prisons, dia-

logue with other religions and in particular Islam), will reinforce the knowledge which the Order has of itself by opening up, on the basis of the concrete reality of the brothers' involvements, the possibility of sharing experiences, of a common pastoral and theological reflection, and of collaborative projects. Up to now little enough real exchange has been undertaken, even if I have often noticed in the course of visitations a need expressed by the brothers to share with others on these themes. I suggest that, in the coming years, the *socius* for the apostolic life should be particularly charged with promoting and animating these exchanges, encouraging the sharing of experience and collaboration, as well as a common reflection. This could contribute progressively to stimulating the apostolic creativity of all.

54. This *creativity of the Order in the service of evangelization* is particularly needed in certain areas and I would like to enumerate here certain questions which have been expressed in the community meetings during the visitations:

o   55. The brothers stress gladly that apostolic creativity ought to be deployed, continuously, in the *simple field of preaching* (parish ministry, pastoral work with young people, the education and promotion of lay people within the Church, the preaching of the Rosary, accompanying popular religious practices, encounter with non-believers) where the cultural, social and ecclesial contexts are in rapid transformation. Along with this, they express also the difficulty represented by the need for mobility because it is not easy to change one's habits, to form oneself for other centers of interest or for other ways of working in view of the needs, to give up an apostolate or a work of which one has come to regard himself as the proprietor, even to change assignation and leave a certain region, to leave work which one loves or a circle of friends. Also, too often, it seems that the time of many of the brothers is given to liturgical pastoral work and in this context it is not easy to respond to new demands. Have we the will to change this state of affairs? We like to talk about mobility even while being aware that we are, in the end, strongly "installed" in established positions. In a globalized world where one values and analyses mobility how are we to find for ourselves the balance between the legitimate need to be established somewhere and the duty of learning how to leave these securities, to "expropriate oneself" in the expression of Benedict XVI?

o 56. In all the provinces I have visited, the brothers consider that the *new networks of communication* are a major challenge for our preaching and that, beyond the new horizons which technical possibilities open up for communication, that there is question here of a new world (a "sixth continent") which the Order must learn to join in order to preach there. In fact the Order has begun to do this: witness the number of brothers on the social networks, for example, as well as one or other more collective initiative. How can we prevent this from individualizing even more each one's preaching? How can we manage together a reflection on the cultural and anthropological challenges of these new networks, in order to exercise there a really creative apostolic encounter?

o 57. The phenomenon of *migration* is a reality that determines the engagements of many provinces, sometimes in specific projects, but also because it is a matter of integrating migrant populations in the pastoral work of parishes, schools, or universities. The reality lived by migrant populations very often reveals the state of the societies that receive them and it cannot leave us indifferent to the priority which the Order ought to give to promoting human rights and justice. We must also be particularly attentive to the question, current today, of why so many migrants, in the course of this difficult experience, leave the Catholic Church. Why does it happen? What is it they are looking for in their Church but are not finding there? How can we identify the help that the Order could/should give to some while accompanying them in their faith? The international reality of the Order could be a particularly valuable resource for developing among us, from country to country, from culture to culture, a sharing of knowledge and collaboration in order to be of support to these populations in ways appropriate to their experience as human beings and as believers.

○ 58. Following the engagement in "peaceful evangelization" of brothers like Bartolomé de Las Casas, *a presence among indigenous populations has an essential place in the history of the Order's preaching.* Certainly, as a result of globalization, and of the mixing and displacement of people into the cities, the situations and modalities of mission have evolved in the course of recent decades, and certain questions (up to now perhaps very "European") have been replaced. The meeting of evangelization with the task of respecting cultural identities, of human development, of social integration, of respect for human rights: this remains crucial in many places. We have the responsibility to follow and to deploy these missions as well as possible so as to transmit the experience we have gained – on the basis of what we have done up to now, but without being tied to that – and to promote the integration into these apostolates of new brothers with their own creativity.

○ 59. Many of our convents are situated in those nerve centers, the *centers of cities.* The conventual (and/or parochial) churches are places of encounter for an extremely diverse population. What might be the contribution of the charism proper to an Order founded precisely in the context of profound urban changes? How might we give the time to listen to the journeys and the human and spiritual searching of this mobile urban population? How might a reflection on the reality of these places, and what they reveal about our societies, aid us in developing a better preaching addressed to the real questions of our contemporaries?

o 60. The great diversity of the Order's foundations means the brothers *encounter other Christian Churches and other religions,* the great religions "of the Book," the religions of Asia, traditional religions, as also diverse currents of searching and of spiritual life. If analyses of the "globalized world" often insist on the process of "secularization," one ought also to underline that the world is really pregnant with religious realities. Faithful to the origins and to the history of the Order, the brothers are already engaged in these dialogues and in efforts toward knowledge. How might we strengthen these further and, especially, how ensure that the preaching of the Order as a whole benefits more from this? It is essential to pursue what has already been undertaken in the area of ecumenism in various parts of the Order, as also in the knowledge of Jewish and Islamic cultures and traditions. Is there place to promote also a reflection on those religions that are called "traditional," especially in Africa? Evoking the time of the Order's foundation, and in the contemporary context, should we not give a greater priority to the worlds and cultures of Islam? The presence of our brothers and sisters in these frontier places of encounter, often marked by difficult human and social realities, and where fragile minorities can be the mediators of peace, ought to be an occasion for a continual renewal of preaching in the Order as a whole. The *"Journées romaines"* (ACG 2010 Rome 164-165) have an important role in this direction.

o 61. Many brothers and communities work in places where the faith is expressed through *pilgrimages and popular devotions.* A number of these realities remind us of the central place in our tradition of the preaching of the Rosary and of the witnesses to holiness. How might the sharing of experiences, and a common reflection, stimulate a pastoral creativity that will not be limited to sacramental accompaniment? What could be the contribution to theological reflection today of the experience lived by many brothers in numerous sanctuaries?

o 62. One line of reflection was dedicated to *"Schools of preaching"* which already take different forms in various provinces and in the Dominican family. The context of the "new evangelization" calls the Order to place its tradition at the service of the Church and to play its part, explicitly and fully, in educating for the announcing of the Gospel, which will include also a reflection on what this consciousness of a necessary renewal of evangelization signifies and represents. It is the responsibility of centers dedicated to it, but also of our institutions of teaching and of research.

o 63. In many provinces the brothers are responsible for *educational institutions* and this ministry is, for the most part, a great joy. They represent for the Order an opportunity to face the challenge of evangelization in the world of young people and of families. The question is often raised of overloading with administrative tasks which prevents a more important engagement in pastoral care or in teaching. How to find a more satisfying balance between these two poles? Many brothers know the particular challenge that is involved in teaching "religion," in competition with the acquisition of pro-fane knowledge and in a context where Christian culture becomes less and less familiar. Here also a common reflection and a sharing of experience will undoubtedly bring much. Is it possible to identify the characteristics of a "Dominican philosophy of edu-cation" which would allow us to develop the apostolic tasks already undertaken and to see what new ones should be founded to respond to the needs we encounter, in particular the needs of the poorest and marginalized populations? In this area of education, it is not beneficial to establish a real collaboration within the Dominican family?

o 64. Some of these themes have already led to the establishment of specialized centers for the study of cultures, societies and religions. These places of knowledge, research and dialogue are fundamental elements in the promotion of study in the Order and it is worthwhile developing yet more concerned with other themes crucial for preaching today. Certainly the number of brothers available is very small for really responding to the needs, but is it not a wonderful opportunity for promoting collaboration among the provinces.

65. In speaking with the brothers about apostolic creativity, *"new foundations"* are often spoken about. In the course of these three years, the Province of Vietnam made foundations in Laos and in Thailand, the Province of the Most Holy Rosary in Myanmar and Timor East, the Province of the Philippines strengthened its new foundation in Indonesia with a new house, the Vice Province of West Africa established a house in Burkina Faso, the foundation of a mission in Equatorial Guinea has proceeded, Equatorial Africa, a vicariate of the Province of France, began a mission in Central African Republic. China remains an essential apostolic challenge. Many Provinces have "missions" established in their own territories and which are essential for them: nevertheless we need to recognize that it is sometimes difficult to mobilize enough brothers to be assigned to them in an ongoing way, as if we prefer to remain in the great urban centers. Here again, whether within or outside the territory of a Province, the challenge is that of mobility. Are we not too "drowsy," at the risk of neglecting this essential missionary dimension of evangelization? What are the important criteria to be honoured so that a new foundation develops the witness of the Dominican life in its fullness? What are the real needs to which we seek to respond when we imagine new missions? There are requests awaiting our response: Madagascar, Zambia, Tanzania, Romania... At the same time. in the North West, the secular context requires missionary inventiveness. Even if we must be realistic and take account of limited

strengths, we cannot forget that *the dynamic of foundation and of the encounter with other cultures is essential to that of evangelization.*

A recurrent question: a specific charism in the Church

66. When I have been in discussion with our communities, the theme of the Order's specific charism is often brought up and the manner in which we can bring *our own contribution to the Church, not only to preserve her as she is, but to participate in her constant work of becoming that which she may be.* I would like to respond to these questions, not with definitive solutions, but rather because such concerns reflect something of the *"statu Ordinis"* today.

67. Whatever the different theories on the subject, (should we, or not, be in charge of parishes?) it is a fact that a large number of brothers, in every region of the Order, is engaged in *parish ministry.* Many point out, quite rightly, that this is a very important place where we can employ the ministry of preaching and can encounter the real life of the Church. Many also say (and this is an answer that can be found among the faithful themselves) that it is important to provide the key characteristic of "Dominican preaching" through this ministry. Based on this, the brothers have many questions. What can we bring to the parish ministry through the witness of the community life that identifies us? What can it bring to the makeup of the parish as a community of be-lievers and more broadly, to the building-up of the Church as communion? In what way could our vocation to preaching make the parishes of which we have charge places from which evangelization spreads through training and forma-tion of the laity? How do we instill more deeply the desire for study at the heart of pastoral work? In what way can we show that mercy is the source of preaching as it is the source of fraternal communion? Do we have a vocation to keep such parishes permanently, or would it not be better, more often, to know when to hand them back to the diocese in order to move into other places or situations that have more need of our presence? Can we undertake a process of systematic

evaluation of our parochial engagements? Where they exist, could the Dominican Priestly Fraternities be an alternative means of the Order's contribution to parish work?

68. In addition to parish responsibilities, many brothers are engaged in *ministries to the local Church* (student, hospital, or prison chaplains, in charge of ecclesial services, accompaniment of various groups) and we should be pleased to provide this service to the particular Churches. It is obvious that, through these ministries, brothers bring our tradition to, and so put the Order at the service of, the life of the Church. Through parishes just as through these specific ministries, we have the opportunity to acquire a deeper knowledge of the ecclesial reality, of the reality of people's lives, their needs and expectations. But fears or regrets are often expressed. Have we too "functionalist" an approach to the office of preaching? Why do we not share more in community about the ministries we have, allowing a deeper community acknowledgement of our needs, perhaps leading us to adjust our priorities better and if necessary, to redefine our apostolic focus? Doesn't the multiplication of individual "contractualised" ministries run the double risk, of the "privatization" of one's preaching, and also of a possible or even accepted lack of mobility? Are we not too caught up in pastoral work for believing assemblies, at the expense of the call to go out and encounter those who do not come often to Church, or even those who have not experienced the Gospel?

69. The reality of our apostolic lives, whether personal or communal, should make us vigilant never to be satisfied with having too personalized or too identified a character. Such reflections on our ministries invite us to evaluate constantly how we seek to *serve the Church of Christ, to promote the desire for communion and to support her efforts to spread to the ends of the earth.*

70. Visiting the Order provides the occasion and the good fortune of meeting brothers engaged in difficult social contexts, forgotten by the "mainstream" of the world (street children, refugees, extreme poverty, those excluded from

society and in precarious labor situations, illness...) They remind us of the priority that the Order places on the promotion of justice and peace. On the margins, these brothers are generally admired, but often considered a little "exotic" among the friars and, if it is a difficult experience for them, such a view carries the risk for us all of being a way to avoid these difficult places. On the one hand, we need to develop further our presence and (collective) links with difficult human and social realities in the world. At the same time, the particularity of "preaching" to the societies with whom we have such links could be an essential means of support. It is in this perspective that we must develop still further the interaction between our presence in the world and the Delegation of the Order to the United Nations (cf. above, the Salamanca Process). This *"preaching to the nations"* is without doubt, one of the ways in which we can implement the heritage received from our predecessors.

71. If the work is not to fail, we cannot neglect the fundamental aspiration of the Order to *"go out to evangelize."* This is certainly an important part of evangelization that helps strengthen the confession, knowledge and practice of the faith in believers. But, in so many places, we notice that the group of believers is much smaller than the group of those who have not yet encountered Christ. How are we to meet them? On which roads, by the side of which wells (as the Message from the Synod on the new evangelization expressed it), upon which Areopagus must we go to walk with them? How can we be truly present with those who leave the Catholic Church to join other communities and how can we enter into dialogue with them? How do we face the fact that in many cultural contexts, the faith is, or has become, foreign? How can we avoid being absorbed by our ministries that, great and important though they are, prevent us from "leaving" the Cenacle to talk with people fortified by the power of the Spirit, so they can hear us and discover, through this meeting, that God speaks to them? What is the apostolic creativity that the Church would be happy to receive from an Order founded by a man whose only desire was to go to the Cumans?

72. So often, discussions reveal that *the most daring freedom for "mobility" of our apostolic creativity confronts several objections or obstacles.* "There are not enough of us," it is often said. But, if is it true that numbers are small, sometimes because we are so dispersed, brothers wait for someone to call them to join a common project or to leave an engagement they have chosen and developed without taking account of the apostolic responsibility of all. Too often, we hesitate to *be summoned to the apostolic life.* "We must keep our historical presences." Some of these are of course very significant. But we must be careful *not to be dominated by the weight of history and its legacies*, which can overwhelm us. Or again, allow ourselves to rest on our laurels, at the expense of an availability to be driven by the current needs and calls. Another obstacle – and it often seems quite tenacious – is that mobility is not without *economic consequences.* Indeed, it is sometimes more this necessity to ensure some "material security" for communities that leads us to choose institutional and intra-ecclesial ministries, with the conviction that what it is about is responding to an apostolic urgency. I have the feeling that this is shared by many other institutes of religious life and that this contributes profoundly, first, to a *loss of recognizability of the charism proper to these Institutes because their members appear principally as resourceful protagonists in the territorial Church*, then, to a *loss of strength in the contribution that the charisms of religious families can make for the universal Church.* From this point of view, I believe that the intuition of St Dominic to send his brothers as mendicants still has something to teach us today.

73. We have *"apostolic institutions"* (schools, universities or formation centers, publishing, apostolate in the world of media...) which allow us to meet certain challenges mentioned above. With other innovative apostolic projects, these institutions often place us on the frontiers of which we speak in our chapters. Six issues are often raised: the demands of a very specific professional competence which corresponds to few of the brothers and weakens our mobility; sometimes the very "worldly" risk of careerism, of

"entrepreneurial passion," or of competitiveness among the brothers; the challenge of the call to give these institutions a Dominican spiritual inspiration; being absorbed by administrative tasks and neglecting community life and prayer; the fragility of economic support; the agreement with lay collaborators, in a true reciprocity.

74. The priories of the Order have often been *places of hospitality for new cultures, for dialogue and intellectual research engaging with other ways of thinking.* At a moment when, in the perspective of the "new evangelization," the relevance of the "Court of the Gentiles" is emphasized, could we give even more force to the initiatives taken by one or other community? It could be a way of serving the "conversation of the world," by making a contribution from the intellectual resources of the Order.

75. Concerning several themes previously mentioned, discussions with brothers often emphasize the importance today of *promoting engagement with laity in evangelization.* This is obviously one of the first goals of every pastoral project in the Church and it is crucial for many brothers dedicated to teaching and formation. But the Order is particularly involved through the Lay Dominican fraternities, the Dominican Youth Movement, the Volunteers, the International Rosary Teams and several lay groups connect to the spirituality and mission of the Order. During my visits, I have confirmed the conviction that our tradition brought us the grace of a real "spiritual family" that we have the responsibility to consolidate even more to put at the service of evangelization. Isn't this reality of the "Dominican Family" a constitutive element of the "specific charism" of the Order?

76. At the end of this chapter dedicated to Preaching, I am expressing the wish that the years in which we are preparing the Jubilee may be the occasion for each entity and each community, by formulating its project of life and mission, to be engaged in a rigorous work of evaluation of the reality of the apostolic life and its necessary adaptations. In eight hundred years, how many new beginnings have there been?

FOUNDING COMMUNITIES

77. "But, what are we going to do there, where you are sending us?," the first friars seemed to ask Dominic. Study, preach and *"found priories:"* it is a dimension of the mission of the Order. Of course, we know that this does not simply mean that we need to found a community when going somewhere, to be able to work for the mission. Sometimes, this distinction blinds us, leading us to consider the life and the communal witness more in an "instrumental" manner, somehow "secondary." When our communities are really working each day to be founded by the engagement of everyone in life with the brothers, they are truly like homes where preaching is rooted in contemplation of the mystery of Christ's friendship with the world; places where the grace of the Spirit transfigures fraternal friendship as a "sacrament" of this friendship of Christ; places, where the light of truth shines, even dimly, which calls and welcomes every seeker of meaning. The experience of fraternal communion is a part of the preaching of the Order.

A practical wisdom of common life

Some risks

78. A *Relatio* should not be naively idealistic and I would like here to point out what seem to me to be the principal risks confronting our communities in the world.

> 79. First, there is the *risk of the "instrumental" community* that favors, or is the result of, the *"privatization" of the apostolic life*. This community becomes one that is only organised along the most "practical" lines possible, neglecting to establish the realities that establish our communities as places of humanity and of the building of fraternity. Places where there is mutual care, not exclusivity, regular chapters, a real common availability of resources, the recognition of our unity made in the same profession of obedience, concretely lived out in just relationships between the prior, each of the brothers and the whole community.

80. The risk of *gentrification* threatens many of our communities and provinces even if it is at different levels in different contexts. Rising standards of living slowly occur and establish themselves until it is no longer possible to live without all the accumulated comforts and securities. At the same time, the distance increases between our way of life and that of people of an average social level and there is a gulf between us, and the poorest of this world. In the same movement, "privatized economies" develop, because this is the way the world works. In too many places, the *"sharing of assets" is a topic of discussion but not a real practice*: "private economies" are developed and an inequality is established between brothers. It is the real practice of the vow that can keep us from getting too attached to the accumulation of personal belongings and so run the risk of division, of false hierarchies among the brothers. This preoccupation should be a major concern and a matter for "correction" without delay.

81. There is the risk of *formalism*, which can make us forget the joy and humanity of simple fraternal relationships if a paramount place is given to the bare observance of our life's structures (which is not without importance for the objectivity of fraternal and spiritual life for one and all). The true places of life and vitality of the brothers are then sought outside of the assigned community.

82. The risk of *communities that are too small*, often multiplied to respond to real apostolic needs, but without allowing for the possibility of all the richness of the fraternal life (prayer, common study, chapters...). The conventual structure (which does not necessarily mean a community of great size) is given to us in the Constitutions as the habitual way of our life, allowing the realization of these aspects.

83. The risk of *immobility* that, sometimes, results in making it impossible to change assignations or to give new ones, so that the balance of the fraternal life is "sedimented" and closed in on itself.

Humanity and wisdom

84. Over the course of the visitations, I have become more and more convinced that we must address ourselves with determination to the issue of the quality of our common life. Too often, *dissatisfaction or frustration at the lack of "human" fraternal relationships* is expressed. Too often, this provokes, or gives the pretext, for the desertion of the fundamental place of our witness and our conversion. Too often, the visitor learns that in this community, no one really talks, that no one is given the minimal conditions to share his faith. Too often, and particularly in very small communities, I notice that it has to take a remarkable energy to resolve tensions due to problems of personal character or psychological difficulties which are never fully confronted, to the detriment of the common engagement in the same apostolic responsibilities.

85. These observations lead me to think that we must seek to cultivate a real *"wisdom of community life."* For this, we have to set aside any opposition between "common life" and "life of mission," for two reasons. First, the witness of a life in search of unanimity is in itself a mission and a proclamation of the Gospel. Secondly, the quality, the density of the common life is what allows people to tap into the source of fraternal communion, the zeal and balance of the mission.

86. This *double dimension, human and spiritual, of our "holy preaching"* must truly demand our attention and summon us to real engagement with each other. It is not only a question of respect for the law (although, the objectivity of the law is indeed the guarantee against each one's own arbitrariness, often that of the "strongest"). It is not a question any longer of introducing a formalism that, beyond structural unity, would reinforce personal rigidities. But it is a question of laying down those necessary conditions for a healthy balance of daily life through which we seek to "live as brothers and be united." The following are some elements that would seem to be indispensable to such a balance. We must refer objectively to the rules of our *Constitutions* that would guarantee the condition of true liberty much better than interpretations and improvements, ending by establishing personal situations or communities that are too banal. Consider *obedience* not as a subject for discussion, an object of negotiation

based upon personal interests, but as the cement that reinforces communion between brothers. *Pray together* daily, listen to the word, celebrate the Eucharist together, share meals, speak, dialogue and be interested in one another, learn to forgive. Such "fundamentals" have an apparent banality, but their absence is too often the source of our decline.

87. Therefore, *our communities need, so often, a practical wisdom to be true places of hope and fraternal communion.* Such wisdom will remind us that our communities should be first of all, communities of faith and celebration, of contemplation, prayer and of listening to the Word of God. It reminds us that they are also places where we can learn to hold in common the apostolic needs of the world. Finally, they should be communities of conversion, where we learn to de-center the self. This practical wisdom emphasizes the necessity for rooting the life of communities, and so, the whole mission of preaching, in the mystery. In view of the Order's Jubilee, it seems to me that each Prior Provincial should discover how to promote such a renewal in his province.

Democracy and communion

88. Democratic life is a true jewel in the tradition of the Order and highlights two challenges: the concrete implementation of the theological reality of fraternity, everyone's voice being sought, promoted and considered in order to define together the common good, supported by all; the witness of such a fraternity at the heart of the structure of contemporary human and social realities.

89. Our democratic life takes form in the chapter, which emphasizes the relationship between individual contribution and the promotion of the common good. We must keep a sense, in particular, of the importance of "representation," which establishes the principle of trust at the heart of capitular life. We should insist upon the search for unanimity in common responsibility for the common good (which is at once fraternal communion, material means, common apostolic responsibility). From this, we can deduce some things: that chapters are important where everyone really gives his thoughts, avoiding focusing upon the "current of opinion" in the corridors: that there needs to be a just relationship between the chapter and council, each

body having its proper role; that Provincial Chapters gather community representatives (priors and delegates of priories), rather than delegates from colleges, something which emphasizes numbers instead of the real situations making up the content of our common responsibility. Continuity in government, which considers the common good, is not accountable to a sequence of alternative choices or ideologies. That a priority is made of the principle of unanimity that is distinguished from a democracy where majority confronts minority. That there is a fair recourse to the superior.

90. Our liturgical celebrations must be at the service of this communion between us, both at the level of communities and of the Order. I like to think of this communion in Santa Sabina, each time I pass the "Prototype," the first liturgical book of our Order, which recalls the essential place our first friars gave to this communion in praise and intercession, because the apostolic zeal of each and everyone drew its strength from the mystery of communion.

Intergeneration

91. The issue of the generations must be considered to take account of the state of the Order.

93. We should not delude ourselves. At the moment, the demography is not balanced in many parts of the Order and, if we are lucky to receive a quite significant number of new brothers, renewal is not guaranteed everywhere. This highlights the importance of a real determination in the promotion of vocations, which would benefit being seen, as far as possible, in synergy with the other members of the Dominican Family. It also points out the attention that we must give to respecting the oldest brothers among us and the support given to them so that their aging may truly be welcomed as a particularly spiritual time and as something that is an aspect of witness to the Gospel that we should make to those societies where the place of the elderly is not always assured.

94. To speak of the passing of generations is to speak of handing things on and in many parts of the Order we must learn to make room for those who are younger, to pass on responsibilities, to avoid the *a priori*. We should trust a new creativity that, having

received a tradition, assumes the true responsibility of an heir, namely, to transform it. The challenge of handing things on is the challenge of a solidarity that on the one hand does not too quickly desert its responsibility under the pretext that "the young must take their turn." But, at the same time, it does not cling to places or positions under the pretext that "the young are not capable."

95. We sometimes hear expressed, here and there in the Order, certain "categorizations" of the younger generations: that they are more traditional, less committed, more emotional, less structured in their faith... I often feel that these quick judgements lead us to avoid welcoming, first of all, the familial, social and professional reality of these young friars. And then, especially, accepting the grace that God gives to the Order through these brothers.

96. We must take care of the oldest brothers. In several provinces, it is a real challenge to know how to provide the most appropriate conditions for the needs of these brothers and, where necessary, the care required for their state of health. But it is also a challenge for us all to learn to live this stage of life without denial or resignation, crediting it with as great a wisdom as possible from the perspective of our human life, both religious and spiritual. I believe that the manner in which we live this age in community can be considered fully part of the witness of the Gospel. Further, in some places, the brothers of the middle generation are few and it is very important to take care to avoid overburdening them: they are sup-porting the oldest while also assuming the task of forming the youngest, while at the same time being expected not to abandon their apostolic work.

Initial Formation

97. In speaking of the generations, we should mention the process of formation. I would like to express three concerns.

98. The first of these is that we must, together, reflect upon requests from the youngest in certain places of the Order who want a stronger, more identified, relationship with tradition. If this is heard and respected, then it is also our common responsibility to pass on the totality of our Order's history, including the manner in which the

brothers over the last decades have sought to face the metamorphoses of the world and the Church: *our security is not in the past but in the future.*

99. The second concern is that we remember that the young friars in the Order are not all made in the same mold, and in particular the worries of young Christians in countries of the North West do not represent all the young of the world: this is to highlight the opportunity that the universal reality of the Order represents.

100. The third is that we reflect properly upon the *process of initiation* that is employed during the initial formation of the brothers. I am worried to see formation done often in a context of a "culture of fear or intimidation," where fear controls the relationships between older and newer friars, a culture where false hierarchies are established, giving in particular, a privileged position to the "priests." The demands of the regular life seem artificial when required of the youngest in initial formation while the oldest are habitually and quite easily dispensed from them. This will lead to habits becoming ingrained, damaging for the vitality and authenticity of the Order.

Acquiring the means for mission

The structure of the entities

101. Following the request of the Rome Chapter, the General Council has undertaken a reflection with the General Vicariates. As Brother Carlos expressed in his *Relatio* at the Chapter in Rome, the Chapter considered it appropriate to take account of the changes of context that have occurred since these vicariates were erected, looking for the direction which would ensure the best mission in these countries and seeking to establish the best conditions for a good balance between apostolic work and the life of the brothers and their communities. The first stage of the study we have begun showed that a certain number of difficulties were common to these entities: a limited number of brothers with the risk of greatly overburdening them with work; administrative structures which are often too cumbersome for a small entity; the fragility of communities, often of small numbers; formation structures that are difficult to set up and with the need to

develop collaborations with other entities; worries about the future based on the limited number of new vocations. Nevertheless, each of these ten vicariates has a particular situation of which we must take account: their own history, their own cultural, ecclesial and social context, and specific issues of the mission of the Order in their country. We have worked from the perspective defined by the Chapter, which envisaged the suppression of the General Vicariates by the year 2016. We propose the three following solutions: becoming a Vice Province; uniting with other entities to make a new entity; becoming a provincial vicariate of another province. I am committed to visiting each of these vicariates. At this point in the process, I would like to make the following remarks:

> 102. The first objective of the process is to ensure the continuation and the deployment of the preaching mission undertaken in these countries and to define the juridical structure most adapted for that; this perspective must remain the goal and constantly be reinforced. Even if, sometimes, some vicariates face real difficulties, all are bearers of the call to preaching in their particularly important specific contexts. The desire to restructure the preaching must not allow us to desert the demands of the mission and the priority which is given to the most difficult places;

> 103. Apostolic restructuring must therefore not be approached first of all in terms of the "category" to which one should belong, but rather establish the objectives and conditions of the preaching;

> 104. To do this, we shouldn't think of an entity only from the point of view of the apostolic work it wants to do, but also, with the same concern, in view of the service to the Order's mission that we want to establish in a place, by means of communities;

> 105. In several cases, a structured collaboration with a province could be sought: the chapter should provide a framework to guide such collaboration;

106. In other cases, entities may consider their autonomy something that demands a program of necessary conditions and a regular evaluation of the process; it belongs to the Chapter to define the methods of participation for these entities in General Chapters;

107. The request to restructure the entities in the Order showed that the reform of General Vicariates made an evaluation of other types of entities necessary. Since it is about strengthening interaction between the conditions of the life of brothers and communities, and the capability for the mission, this process would develop collaborations. We should thus specify how the "stronger" provinces might bring their contribution in an organised fashion. Some provinces are very fragile and there are few precise determinations in our laws to deal with "decline." Some Provincial Vicariates do not fulfill the minimum conditions to achieve the autonomy corresponding to their status. In certain provinces, it is essential to rethink what is a just relationship between "province" and "vicariate:" these relationships are not only of an economic type and can no longer be simple dependence; a province must make every effort to be stimulated in its own life and local mission by the fact that it has responsibility for a vicariate. In continuing this reform of our structures, we must thus reflect on: the status of a Provincial Vicariate and its status within a province and its government; the method of accompanying very fragile entities or entities in decline and the framework for collaboration with other entities; the status of house of a province in the territory of another, their meaning and current goals. In this reflection, and because, thanks be to God, the Order's life is today a global dynamic, it is not a question only of setting out the hierarchy of the entities, but rather, of thinking how we can ensure the implementation of the mission.

The work of the Curia

108. You will understand that this restructuring makes sense in the perspective of the renewal of our charism of evangelization, inspired by the celebration of the Order's Jubilee. With the Council, we have drawn up some guidelines that could be used to organise this celebration, wanting the dynamism of the Jubilee to animate every level of the Order's life. In continuity with the novena of preparation begun by Brother Carlos, on the basis of these reflections, I asked Brother José Gabriel Mesa to present to the Chapter an approach and possible agenda for this celebration of the Jubilee. I hope the Chapter will be the occasion to invite the Order and the Dominican Family, at every level, to enter into the process of the Jubilee.

109. Responding to the request of the Rome Chapter, the policy of communication and promotion of the media has been restructured, unified under the responsibility of the General Promoter of the Media. This has already taken the form of the construction of a new Order website, based upon an interactive network of brothers from different regions, and a new form of IDI (International Dominican Information). The next step should be the setting up of an internet network to facilitate communication between the Order's brothers and the promotion of preaching on social networks.

110. Two regions, Italy and Malta, and the Iberian Peninsula, now have one *socius*. So, currently, there are seven regional *socii* (United States, Latin America and the Caribbean, Asia-Pacific, Africa, Southern Europe, Central and Eastern Europe, Western Europe and Canada). Echoing the "triple-sending" of Dominic, I would like the Chapter to allow the *Master of the Order to appoint a supplementary "transversal" socius who, along with those appointed to the apostolic and intellectual life, would be dedicated to "community life."* He would have the particular job of following the process of restructuring undertaken in several entities, but also to promote with Provincials, the consolidation of our communities (networks of cooperator brothers in the Order, liturgical life, permanent formation, aging). At the moment, aspects of the Order's life are each assigned to a particular *socius*: initial formation,

Dominican Family, cooperator brothers, contact for the International Liturgy Commission, the session for new Provincials, the Dominican Youth Movement. After the Chapter, the Council will reorganise these responsibilities for the next three years.

111. There has been a development in the *method of canonical visitations* undertaken in the provinces. Studying the directives suggested by the Chapter, the General Council has finally chosen to use two types of canonical visitation – one that takes the time to visit a whole province and the other dedicated more to *the evaluation of the progress made since the last visit or to studying with the brothers certain specific issues for the entity*. The goal is to facilitate the continuity between these visits and to favor the possibility of working in common with the provinces, according to the particular needs of each entity. We must continue to co-ordinate these visits with the work done throughout the year by the *socii* and promoters. Further, in a habitual way, the visits act as communal meetings through which, such exchanges between brothers are the occasion to learn better the apostolic realities of a province and to notice the principal issues in the common apostolic responsibility, as well as supporting its creativity.

112. At each plenary meeting of the General Council (now four times a year), a meeting of the Promoters is held with the aim of strengthening coordination between us all.

113. The Chapter of Rome asked that a Congress of the Order be prepared, dedicated to the *vocation of the cooperator brother*. The General Council, backed by a small coordinating commission, set up a reflection by the cooperator brothers themselves at a regional level. This process included, last November, on the anniversary of the canonization of Martin de Porrès in Lima, a meeting of fifty cooperator brothers from the different regions of the Order. This meeting helped to identify certain points of which the ongoing reflection should take note and directions to be specified: the clear recognition by all of the distinction in the Order of two

specific vocations, to be called to be a friar preacher as a priest, and to be called to be a friar preacher as a co-operator; the struggle against the tendency to attribute a superiority of the first over the second; in this, the need to promote in the Order the meaning of the witness of fraternal life, the meaning of the mystery of fraternity; an evaluation of the tendencies that we can have to think of religious life, and sometimes to set hierarchies between us, out of clerical categories; the necessity of promoting the cooperator brother vocation, fully integrated in the vocations promotion of the Order; the specific clarification of a program of studies, taking care to adapt this process according to the diversity of the brothers presenting themselves as cooperators; the participation of a cooperator brother in the promotion of vocations and the accompaniment of formation; the training of masters of formation so that they may have a profound knowledge of the expectation of the Order concerning the specific vocation of the cooperator brother; a deeper reflection in the Order upon the spiritual sources of the Order and its "mystery;" the development of lay ministries at the heart of the Order; the promotion and support of the apostolic creativity of cooperator brothers. These themes will now be studied in regional groups and then I would like their reflection to be passed on for study in each entity.

114. In terms of the *economic life of the Order*, conforming to the requests of the Chapter, a professional annual evaluation is scheduled for the accounts of the Curia and an "Investment Evaluation Commission" has been set up by the Economic Council. In connection with the Syndic of the Order, each entity is asked to establish systematically the same type of evaluation and assessment. The same request must be made to the Institutions under the direct jurisdiction of the Master.

115. The appointment of a *Solidarity Board* that will accompany entities in their projects, will promote a strong culture of solidarity among us, will reorganise different existing funds, and will use certain means to fundraise. At the same time, on the basis of already accomplished work, and being precisely dedicated to projects of the Order set by the

General Council (currently, the École Biblique, the Angelicum, and IDEO), IDF is committed to clarifying its goals and means. I would like this solidarity to follow at least two priorities: the support of initial formation in entities for whom it is difficult to do this alone, and the support of the most fragile entities.

The Dominican Family

116. The call to "found communities" should make us consider the reality of the Dominican Family, and how we, the friars, are involved.

117. During my visits to the provinces, I have met certain *communities of nuns*, without it being possible to visit every community. However, following in the footsteps of my predecessors, it seems to me that the Master of the Order should make it a real priority, and so make time, for the Nuns of the Order. Their monastic life, dedicated to contemplation and completely given to the Word of God, is a leaven for the life and preaching of the entire Order, just as it is an essential aspect of Dominican preaching in the world. While it is hard to see very fragile communities in some regions, we can also rejoice that projects for new foundations grow or come to birth. In order to know better, and to study this aspect of the Order's mission with the nuns, as well as the way in which this mission is joined to the particularity of Dominican monastic life, I have already met a good number of Federations or Assemblies (Spain, Italy, Mexico, Peru, USA, France, Eastern Europe). In collaboration with the International Commission for Dominican Nuns, and these Federations, I would like the sisters to help me identify points on which to support them, while respecting the autonomy of each monastery. For this, we would have a common reflection upon some themes: the connection of the autonomy of each monastery with the global dynamic of the entire Order, communication between the two authoritative branches of the Holy See and the Master of the Order's own responsibility in respect of the Nuns, the job of the Promoter for the Nuns, the link with the whole of the Dominican Family,

collaboration for initial formation, identification of minimal conditions for the maintenance of an autonomous community and the discernment of decisions to close, the following of canonical procedures, the possibilities offered for distance learning, responsibility for solidarity funds between monasteries, accompanying the elderly... We know well, in some regions of the world Dominican monastic life is becoming fragile. Of course, it would be good to see how we can help communities in difficulty and it is obvious that a reorganization of the nuns' presence is essential in some regions. But because fundamentally the Order's mission needs the presence of the nuns, I think that, where it is necessary, the whole Order must be committed to promote this vocation and its deployment, to avoid letting necessary closures or regrouping be the only determining element: a future vision of the presence and mission of the nuns must be set out without delay. This renewal is, of course, the primary responsibility of the nuns themselves but, because it falls under the working out of the Order's mission as a whole, I would like the sisters, friars, and the Dominican Family also, to reflect upon the issue.

118. During visits to the provinces, we try to make time to meet the Dominican Family. This allows us to experience the *real dynamism of the Lay Dominican fraternities* in many places and which take many different forms. I am emphasizing particularly the commitment to a stronger and stronger engagement of the Dominican laity in the mission of evangelization, either through the involvement of members, sustained by fraternal life, in various types of apostolate or ministries, or through apostolic projects undertaken in common. This aspect of the Order's life seems to me to need constant support and reinforcement, for it places the Order in the evolution of the Church's life as it currently is. This suggests that we recognise the knowledge and mutual esteem between the various members of the Dominican Family. This is a prerequisite for the emergence of genuine collaboration, where everyone, without pretensions of grandeur, exercises his own qualities. Here and there, we must acknowledge that, the friars, restrained perhaps by lack

of time, insufficient knowledge or, sometimes, a certain "clericalism," are not always the most spontaneously open to this point of view.

119. *Other lay groups belong to the Dominican Family* and the challenges with which evangelization is faced certainly call for a strengthening and development of this aspect of our family. In this framework, two movements in particular are found: the Volunteer movement, which still needs to be strengthened and considered more like a possible collaboration through the friars; the Dominican Youth Movement, which is, in my opinion, very precious for promoting engagement with the young for evangelization and for which the next assembly will confirm the statutes, structures and goals for the coming years. Further, as my predecessors have often expressed, the promotion of the role of the laity in evangelization must bring us to even more creativity in developing new forms of participation for lay groups in our mission and so expanding the Dominican Family.

120. The report to the Chapter from Sr Fabiola, President of DSI, will give information on the reality and dynamism of the *Apostolic Dominican Sisters*. I would only like to point out here the richness of collaboration with the sisters and our common responsibility to promote the role of women in evangelization.

121. An *International Board of the Dominican Family* has been set up. Once a year it brings together representatives from Dominican Lay Fraternities, the International Commission of the Nuns, Dominican Secular Institutes, Priestly Fraternities, and Apostolic Sisters (DSI). It could be extended to the Dominican Youth Movement, to volunteers, and to other affiliated groups.

122. At the end of this *Relatio*, allow me to mention once more the coming celebration of the anniversary of the Order's confirmation in three years time. The present Chapter will certainly invite the Order to prepare and carry out this celebration. In doing so, I hope it invites us really to consider this Jubilee as the chance to draw once more from

the source of our charism, setting our footsteps in those of St Dominic, friend of Christ, friend of human beings.

ACTIONS – PAGES

TOPICAL INDEX

Dominican Youth Movement, v, 21, 33, 50, 129, 140, 144
DSI, 144
DYM, v, 50
dynamic of formation, 3
EBAF, 8, 34
École Biblique, v, 34, 43, 116, 142
electronic voting, 67
entities, vii, 18, 41, 42, 50, 52, 56, 58-64, 67-71, 76, 92, 102, 104, 109, 136, 138, 139, 141
evangelization, 3, 4, 12, 25, 27, 100, 101, 104, 107, 108, 111, 113, 114, 117, 118, 119, 121, 123, 124
formalism, 131
Formators, 52
fraternal visits, 18
Friars Preachers, 25
Funds, 68
general council, 69, 84, 87, 90, 100, 111
General Council, 59, 66, 68, 71, 95, 136, 140, 142
general curia, 100
General Curia, 4, 28, 68, 71, 72, 96
General Promoter for Communication, 50
General Promoter of the Media, 139
general vicariate, 3, 6, 59, 60, 70, 72, 74, 77, 85, 136, 137, 138
gentrification, 131
'*Go and tell my brothers!*': Dominicans and evangelization, 18
holy preaching, 3, 26, 132
I.D.I., 18, 139
IDEO, 142
IDF, 69, 71, 142
IDYM, 33
immobility, 131
inchoate, 60, 63
Inquisition, 29
Instituto Storico Ordinis Praedicatorum, 29
International Board of the Dominican Family, 144
International Liturgical Commission, 35, 140
International Rosary Teams, 129
Internet, v, 4, 30, 33, 50, 66

Intranet, 118, 139
Investment Evaluation Commission, 141
Islam, 119, 122
ISOP, 29
itinerancy, 23, 30, 105
Jewish, 122
JIP, 64
Journées Romaines Dominicaines, 50
Jubilee, iv, v, 1, 2, 5, 14, 18, 23-25, 28, 30-32, 34, 40, 44, 47, 58, 59, 61, 100, 101, 108, 113, 117, 118, 129, 133, 139, 145
Las Casas, 9, 113, 121
'*Laudare, Praedicare, Benedicere.*', 18
Lay Fraternities, vi, 67, 129, 144
LCO, 16, 58, 73, 74, 96
LCO 1, § VI, 57
LCO 59 § II, 35
LCO 63, 35
LCO 66 § I, 35
LCO 76, 40
LCO 83, 109
LCO 91, 40
LCO 91-2, 41
LCO 159, 75
LCO 164-176, 54
LCO 208, 94
LCO 217-220, 58
LCO 247 § II, 76
LCO 251-bis, 52
LCO 251-ter, 52
LCO 252, 59, 63
LCO 252-256, 74
LCO 253 § I, 60
LCO 257, 61
LCO 257 § I, 60
LCO 257 § I, 1°, 60, 64
LCO 258 § I, 60
LCO 260 § II, 74
LCO 270 § III, 94
LCO 270 and 271, 96
LCO 271 § III, 92
LCO 297-bis, 95
LCO 32 § II, 38
LCO 345, 59
LCO 362 § IV, 62
LCO 384 § II, 1°, 62
LCO 391, 6°, 92, 93, 96

* 9 7 8 1 6 2 3 1 1 0 1 7 8 *